The Hunter's Bible

Revised Edition

The Hunter's Bible
Revised Edition

W. K. Merrill and Clair F. Rees

DOUBLEDAY
NEW YORK LONDON TORONTO SYDNEY AUCKLAND

PUBLISHED BY DOUBLEDAY

a division of Bantam Doubleday Dell Publishing Group, Inc.
666 Fifth Avenue, New York, New York 10103

DOUBLEDAY and the portrayal of an anchor with a dolphin
are trademarks of Doubleday, a division of Bantam Doubleday Dell
Publishing Group, Inc.

Library of Congress Cataloging-in-Publication Data
Merrill, W. K. (Wilfred Kerner), 1903–
The hunter's bible.
ISBN 0-385-17219-2
  Includes appendices: Where to write for hunting
  information—Ballistics tables.
  1. Hunting. I. Rees, Clair F. II. Title.
SK33.M55   1986   799.2   85-30736

Contents

6   Contents

1

The Adventure of Modern Hunting

Hunting today is a sport many millions of people enjoy. Men and women from all walks of life buy hunting licenses every year, while increasing numbers of youths enroll in hunter safety classes to qualify for licensing when the right birthday arrives.

More people hunt today than at any other time in history. In many parts of the country work comes to a virtual standstill when hunting season begins. Schools and factories may shut down for a holiday as entire communities head for the deer woods. Duck hunters arise well before dawn to get a few hours of gunning in before driving to the office, and on fall weekends the countryside teems with pheasant and quail hunters.

In the face of pressure from small but vocal anti-hunting groups, hunting remains firmly entrenched as our number one personal partic-

ipation sport. Long a national pastime, its popularity continues to grow.

Why do men and women enjoy hunting? At one time men hunted from necessity. Less than a century ago a hunter returning empty-handed often meant no meat on the table, and our primitive ancestors obtained not only food, but also clothing and shelter solely through their hunting skills. At one time, man was forced to hunt merely to survive.

That is no longer the case for most of us. Supermarkets carry every kind of food imaginable, and even a standing rib roast of the finest beef is less costly than most game bagged afield. If hunting was a matter of simple economics, sporting goods stores would soon close *en masse* and the deer woods would quickly empty.

Today's sportsman hunts for the pure plea-

Men and women both enjoy hunting. Diminutive nimrod Elaine Brooks with an 8½-foot Alaskan grizzly she shot.

sure of the sport. Even if he returns without any game, he likely has a fine time. As a matter of fact, many nimrods purposely reduce their chances of success by using short-range handguns or primitive weapons like bows and arrows and muzzle-loading rifles in their pursuit of game. Very few of these hunters succeed, but they would rather test their woodsmanship and stalking skills than use a modern, long-range rifle.

The thrill of the chase adds pleasure to the hunt. Many outdoorsmen enjoy pitting their civilization-blunted senses against a wild animal's survival instincts. Stripped of computers and other tools of our technically oriented, highly integrated society, the hunter must depend on himself alone. He learns satisfying self-reliance, and exercises muscles and brain cells long allowed to lie dormant. There's satisfaction, too, in eating meat obtained by individual skill and effort. As a bonus, properly prepared game is both distinctive and delicious.

Why do hunters hunt? They enjoy the adventure of being outdoors, and take delight in the animals around them. The hunting instinct is inherited, and lies buried within most of us, no matter how deeply. Thousands of years ago only the good hunters survived, and that gene still lives. We may no longer *need* to hunt—we simply *want* to. For that matter, the need to hunt—the need to escape our crowded, fast-paced cities and periodically spend some time leisurely walking the woods and rediscovering nature's wonders—was likely never more real. For many, the need to hunt is the need to relax and enjoy life.

Where to Hunt

Though the public lands available for hunting continue to shrink, there are many excellent hunting areas still available. With a few queries and a little careful planning, almost anyone can find productive hunting within a short drive from home. Whitetail deer are found in woods and farmland close to many large cities, while fine waterfowling exists within sight of skyscrapers and grain silos alike. Hunting pheasants, grouse, and other upland game may require you to drive to another county and ask a farmer's permission to trespass, but even this pursuit seldom involves long distances.

Rabbits and squirrels are ubiquitous, while foxes and other predators sure to be nearby provide their own brand of hunting excitement. In the spring and summer months, ground squirrels, marmots, and other rodents swarm grassy pastures and attract riflemen from miles around.

No matter where you live in the United States, there's good hunting nearby. To learn what and where to hunt, the first step is to call your state wildlife representative. Wildlife (or game and fish) offices are maintained in most medium to large cities, and they employ information officers specifically for the purpose of

Many hunters purposely reduce their chances of success by using primitive weapons like bows and arrows. The added challenge increases their pleasure.

passing "where and when to go" advice on to you, the sportsman. This information is as close as your telephone.

Many newspapers publish regular outdoor columns containing hunting tips and advice, as well as current information as to where you're likely to have success. National sports magazines provide a similar service, but the hunting news you learn from your local newspaper is more valuable and more timely when it comes to locating nearby gunning sites.

Another excellent source for up-to-date localized information is the sporting goods store you buy your equipment from. Both clerks and customers are likely to know where the hunting is currently best, although don't expect pinpoint directions to their favorite, secret

While public lands available for hunting continue to shrink, there are many excellent hunting areas still available. (BRENT HERRIDGE PHOTO)

grouse cover. Once you find which part of the county is bringing success, you're on your own. When you've done all the detective work you can in advance, it's time to go afield and locate your own birds, rabbits, or deer.

If you want to travel farther afield to hunt game not locally available, you simply need to make plans well in advance. A trip west to hunt antelope or trophy mule deer requires more preparation than needed for a cottontail hunt across the county line, but there are plenty of resources readily available to ensure your success. No one can guarantee that you'll bag your game; however, if you'll ask the right

people the right questions and plan ahead, you can make sure you'll have a totally enjoyable hunt. The fact that you may live hundreds of miles from large game shouldn't prevent you from being in the right place at the right time, and having a fine time.

Again, contacting the game and fish or wildlife conservation office in the state you plan to hunt is a logical first step. A letter or telephone call should get you the basic information you need to begin: the season opening and closing dates, most productive areas, license costs and application deadlines, and regulations regarding firearms and loads. The wildlife informa-

Guides and outfitters are recommended and even required in some areas. For high, backcountry going, an outfitter's pack string is the only transportation. (U.S. FOREST SERVICE)

ion office should also be able to give you a list of professional guides and outfitters, if necessary.

In some states, like Alaska, guides are required for nonresidents who intend to hunt certain species. If you plan to travel north for moose or grizzlies, a competent outfitter often means the difference between hunting success and failure.

Professional guides are costly, but having the services of someone who knows the country and has a good idea of where game is located is always an excellent idea. Planning for the hunt is covered at greater depth in the next chapter, but the availability of local expertise can be a factor that may help you decide just *where* to hunt next fall.

Excellent public hunting is available on Bureau of Land Management (BLM) and Forest Service land, and these agencies can often be helpful in learning where to go. Detailed topographic maps are available from the sources listed in Appendix 1.

There are many private hunting clubs in operation throughout the United States, and membership ensures you of a regular place to hunt. A few national clubs offer facilities in several different states, and this eliminates possible trespass problems. There are also combination hunting clubs and game farms where you can shoot upland game for a fee. Because the birds you shoot on these establishments are privately raised, season opening and closing dates and certain other state game laws may not apply. This lets you enjoy extending your hunting activities well beyond the dates stipulated for public hunting.

Information about shooting preserves and hunting clubs is available from The National Shooting Sports Foundation, Inc., 1075 Post Road, Riverside, CT 06878. Or check your local Yellow Pages under "Hunting Preserves."

You needn't join a private club or pay a per-bird fee to hunt. Most federally owned land is open to public hunting, and there are public hunting grounds in or near many national game refuges. For example, the Bear River Refuge in Utah has certain areas set aside for

There are public hunting grounds in or near many national game refuges. For instance, Utah's Bear River Migratory Bird Refuge has certain areas set aside for public gunning, and it is a top waterfowling spot.

public gunning, and it is one of the top migratory waterfowl hunting areas in the Intermountain West. Similarly, the Mattamuskeet, in North Carolina, has become one of the most famous goose-shooting areas of the Atlantic coast. Here the state fish and game department manages the public shooting under a cooperative agreement with the U.S. Fish and Wildlife Service. Portions of the Bowdoin and Medicine Lake in Montana, Deer Flat in Idaho, Havasu and Imperial along the Arizona and Imperial along the Arizona and California borders, the Lower Klamath and Tule lakes in California, Ruby Lake in Nevada, the Snake River in Idaho, and the Upper Mississippi extending through Minnesota, Wisconsin, Illinois, Iowa, and Missouri furnish public shooting for waterfowl. Those are a few examples; chances are, similar public shooting grounds are available in your own state.

The Future of Hunting

Industrial development and encroaching civilization have inevitably taken their toll of lands available for wildlife. Some species, like sage grouse and grizzly, are intolerant of man's intrusion. They can't comfortably coexist with man, and where oil rigs and subdivisions appear, this game leaves forever.

Fortunately, other animals are far more adaptable. Both mule and whitetail deer not only survive, but thrive in relatively close proximity to civilization, and the wily coyote includes such unlikely places as Hollywood Boulevard in its habitat. Pheasants and quail depend on man-planted food for much of their diet, and these birds turn up in some surprising places.

The hunting scene has changed in the last few decades. Game laws are stricter, and bag limits have often been reduced. Many privately owned lands have been placed "off limits" to hunters and other sportsmen in response to unthinking acts of vandalism, while other hunting areas now house real estate developments.

At the same time, professional game managers have been successful in keeping high quality hunting available to vast numbers of sportsmen. Organizations like Ducks Unlimited have raised money to buy up prime Canadian marshland in waterfowl breeding areas, and today's nimrod knows more about conservation than his father or grandfather did. Game

Thanks to careful management, some game is more plentiful than ever and other popular species have been imported from abroad. The Chinese ringneck, our most popular upland game bird, is such a transplant.

Encroaching civilization is taking a toll among species like sage grouse, which are intolerant of man's intrusion. Where oil rigs or subdivisions appear, such game leaves forever.

hogs still exist, but their numbers are dwindling.

Some game, like mule deer, is actually more plentiful than it was at the turn of the century, thanks to careful management and hunting controls. In several parts of the country, game herds have been established in huntable numbers in areas where the animals had never before existed. Grouse, moose, mountain goats, and sheep have been transplanted successfully, and exotic game from Africa and Asia can now be hunted in Texas and other states. For that matter, our most famous and popular upland game bird, the Chinese pheasant, isn't native to these shores.

Today's hunter pays considerably more for his sport than he did a few decades ago. Licensing costs have inevitably risen, and fees for professional guide services can be substantial. Guns, ammunition, and other gear are more expensive due to inflation, and with rising fuel prices even driving to the hunting ground costs more these days.

At the same time, the sportsman's income has risen, and he has more leisure time to enjoy his sport. On the average, he's far better educated than his predecessors were, and he understands the need for game management and conservation. He also understands the need to keep hunting alive in this country, and makes this conviction known to legislators.

Hunting is different than it was in the 1920s and '30s. In some ways it's better. With luck and intelligent action, sport hunting will be available to our grandchildren, and *their* grandchildren as well. Hunting *isn't* simply the killing of wild game. It's relaxation, and the enjoyment of nature at its fullest. Hunting was once the most important survival tool man possessed. As fulfilling recreation, it may be equally important to man's survival today.

2

Planning the Hunt

The preceding chapter gave some basic "where to hunt" information, primarily to give you a taste of the type and variety of hunting available in this country. Depending on the quarry you're after, you can hunt nearby and be home in time for supper, or you can travel thousands of miles and spend several days or weeks in the primitive back country.

The kind of hunting you do will depend on your taste, the time you have available, and your pocketbook. Almost every deer hunter would like to travel north to Alaska or cross the border into Canada to try his (or her) luck on larger game. Similarly, many upland game gunners long to travel to Nebraska or some other midwestern state to sample the fabled pheasant hunting available there. Hunters aren't immune to "the grass is always greener" syndrome, and in some cases this feeling is justified. Where else but Alaska can a sportsman

pit his wits against the giant coastal grizzly or locate a moose wearing 75-inch antlers? If you want elk, you *must* travel west, and pronghorn are found in only a handful of states.

At the same time, there's good hunting available throughout the United States, and almost anyone can find plenty of sport close to home. Rabbits and squirrels are found almost everywhere, and whitetail, blacktail or mule deer can be hunted within a half-day drive (or less) of any point on the map. Waterfowling is better in some states than in others, but you can hunt ducks or geese successfully in most parts of the country.

If you're a beginning hunter, or have recently moved to an area you haven't yet had the chance to explore, a quick call to the state wildlife conservation or game and fish office will quickly let you know exactly what game is available nearby. Such offices can be found in

If hunting close to home doesn't provide sufficient adventure, you can travel thousands of miles and spend days or weeks in primitive backcountry. (U.S. FOREST SERVICE)

You can hunt ducks or geese successfully in most parts of the country, and other kinds of gunning can almost always be found close to home.

most medium-sized cities, with their headquarters located in the state capital.

The Importance of Advance Planning

Unless you live in one of the half-dozen most densely populated areas in the country, you should be able to find a fair amount of game you can hunt on day trips from your home. Obviously, for this kind of hunt only minimal planning is needed. You only need to awaken early enough to have the time necessary to travel to the intended hunting site and arrive before dawn, when the best hunting almost invariably occurs. If the route is unfamiliar, sketch it in advance on a state road map and make sure you know where the turnoffs are. Allow yourself extra time if you plan to eat breakfast en route, and gas up the car the night before.

If you intend to hunt on farmland or other private property, you can save valuable time and possible frustration by obtaining trespass permission in advance. This means you should take the time to visit the area several days *before* the hunt and become acquainted with property owners. While farmers and ranchers are increasingly leery of allowing gun-toting strangers on their land, a polite approach and a straightforward request for hunting permission usually pays off. But the time to get such permission *isn't* before daybreak on the season opener. Meet the farmer at a decent hour a week or so before you plan to hunt, and reassure him that you won't hunt near his cattle or walk on his unharvested crops. Promise to close gates behind you—and then see that you *keep* those promises during the hunt. Every ranching and farming businessman has had unpleasant experiences with "sportsmen" who

Deer can be hunted within a half-day drive or less of almost any point on the map in the United States. (MAINE DEPARTMENT OF ECONOMIC DEVELOPMENT)

your pump or auto shotgun is plugged to limit the capacity of the gun to only three shots. Failure to do so is a common oversight, and one that can be both embarrassing and expensive if you meet a game warden.

For most kinds of hunting, the family car or station wagon will suffice as transportation. But if you'll be traveling in the mountains, particularly in late fall, a four-wheel-drive pickup truck or utility car offers greater peace of mind. If snow can be expected, a set of chains is good insurance. Make sure the battery and tires are in good condition, and see that there's enough antifreeze in the radiator. Hunting deer in the high country can drop the temperature a good twenty degrees. Battery jumper cables and a tow chain are worthwhile additions on a rough-country hunt, and a shovel often comes in very handy.

If you plan on traveling a long way from home for a more extended hunt, you'll have a longer checklist. If you'll be driving your own car, you simply need to take more food and maybe an extra change of clothing or two.

failed to properly respect his property, and that's why so many gates are closed to hunters today. But if you appear to be a responsible individual and have the courtesy to ask in advance, chances of obtaining permission to hunt remain pretty good. If a landowner *does* turn you down, don't argue—simply thank him for his time and drive up the road to the *next* farmhouse you see. Persistence pays off, but make sure it's *polite* persistence.

For a one-day hunt, most of the other preparations are a matter of simple, common sense. Be sure to buy the required license and—where required—game stamps, and bring your gun and an ample supply of the right kind of ammunition. If you'll be hunting migratory waterfowl or doves, make sure the magazine of

When hunting on private property, be sure to obtain permission in advance. Then respect fences and other private property. (MAINE DEPARTMENT OF ECONOMIC DEVELOPMENT)

Kimber .22 bolt rifle makes a top choice for hunting small game. Leupold 4X scope improves chances at extended range.

Getting Your Bearings

For weekend hunts in populated rural areas, a simple road map should supply all the directions you need. But if you're headed for the deer woods or the western desert, you should obtain a topographical map of the area. Sources for such maps are listed in Appendix 1. You'll also need a compass to help you orient the map. Map and compass use will be discussed in a later chapter.

One of the smartest things any sportsman can do before hunting deer or other large game in a new or unfamiliar area is to do a little advance scouting. Drive to the area a few weeks in advance and spend a day walking through it. Learn the lay of the land. Compare the terrain with that map you should have acquired. Check the condition of the browse nearby and look for probable feeding and resting areas. Look for fresh signs and heavily traveled deer trails. Don't be fooled by an *old* deer trail, incidentally. If you can't find fresh

tracks, the deer may be somewhere else on the mountain. While you're there, locate a couple of likely ambush points for your opening-morning stand. That'll put you well ahead of the game when you and your party arrive exhausted in camp the evening before the season begins.

That brings up another point. If at all possible, plan your trip so that you can arrive in camp no later than early afternoon the day before the hunt—or, better yet, the day before *that.* That will give you time to get camp properly set up and everyone a chance to do some advance scouting. If you know exactly where to go that first morning of the hunt, you'll better than treble your odds for success.

Keeping Warm

Warm clothing and sturdy but *not* brand-new boots should be worn for most kinds of hunting. Blaze-orange or "hunter orange" outer clothing is almost universally required for hunting deer and may be stipulated for upland game hunting as well. Check your state game laws if you have any questions about this.

Waterfowlers should wear appropriate footwear—hip boots or waders—and don wind- and waterproof camouflaged outer clothing. Don't forget such niceties as warm underwear and gloves. Sitting motionless in a duck blind can be cold work if you fail to dress warmly enough. Even for an overnight hunt, a change or two of wool socks is needed. If there's a chance of rain or snow, an extra pair of pants and a spare shirt is a good idea.

Lunch is a matter of personal taste, but hot chocolate, coffee, or some other warming beverage in a vacuum bottle is always welcome on frosty mornings.

Overnight or weekend forays afield are only slightly more complicated. You need some kind of shelter (tents are inexpensive and do a fine job if you don't have access to a pickup-mounted camper or small trailer), a good sleeping bag, and a ground cloth and mattress to keep the bag warm and dry.

Half the fun of hunting deer lies in spending the night in the woods, and you don't have to drive 30 miles to start hunting when you wake up in the morning. (U.S. FOREST SERVICE)

Food and Cookware Provisions

For cooking, a white-gas or butane-powered camp stove is nice, or you can do a pretty good job by using the embers of the campfire. Cast-iron cookware is a favorite of outdoor chefs; it's rugged, easy to clean (simply wipe it out with a paper towel before it cools), and retains heat well for even cooking.

Be sure to bring plenty of water along unless you know for certain it will be available where you plan to camp. Your menu can be as simple or as fancy as you like. Eggs, bacon, and steaks are easy to cook, or you can go the beans and hamburger route. Disposable paper or plastic plates reduce cleanup chores but become im-

practical for any kind of extended camping trip. Don't forget a roll of tinfoil and another of paper towels—these items are indispensable in a hunting camp kitchen.

Plan your grocery list so you can buy most of the perishable items when you're close to the hunting area. This will keep your car a few pounds lighter on the trip in, and save on ice. Just make sure you don't forget that final provisioning stop before you arrive in camp. Longer hunting trips also increase the likelihood of sickness or accident, so bring along a first aid kit and a few favored antibiotics. Don't forget aspirin and anti-diarrhea remedies. Toilet paper is also nice to have on hand, but paper towels will do in a pinch.

The smartest thing a hunter new to an area can do is to scout the terrain in advance. (BRENT HERRIDGE PHOTO)

Motel or Camping Out

If you're hunting upland game or waterfowl, you can probably arrange to spend the night at a nearby motel. Be sure to make reservations well in advance, as such facilities have a way of filling up early in prime hunting areas. Sleeping at a motel and eating your meals in restaurants greatly simplifies your planning list— simply bring plenty of money or credit cards.

For real wilderness hunting, camping out offers many advantages. Half of the fun of hunting deer lies in spending the night in the woods, and you don't have to drive thirty miles to start hunting when you wake up in the morning. Deciding whether to rough it or spend each night on a motel mattress between clean sheets is part of the planning process. The decision is up to you and the people you'll be hunting with. But it's a decision that should be made early; your other plans hinge on it.

Traveling by Plane

If you're flying to a distant state (or country) to hunt with an outfitter, chances are you'll only need to bring your personal items. This includes your own clothing, sleeping bag, mat-

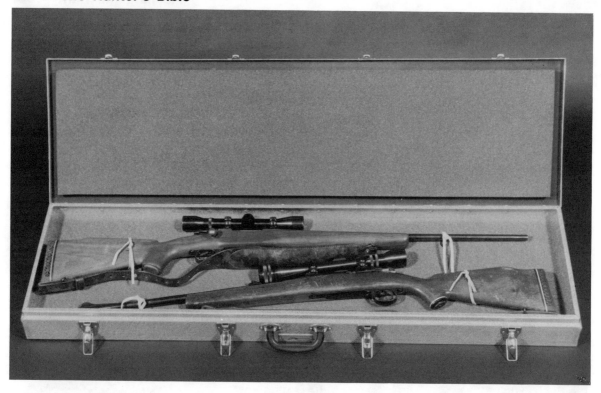

The best bet for shipping firearms as airline baggage is a hard aluminum luggage-type container like this Saf-T-Case rifle case.

tress, toilet gear, rifle, ammunition, binoculars, and personal effects. Check with your outfitter in advance to see what items of gear he normally provides, and what items *you'll* be responsible for. If you'll be flying to camp in a bush plane or horsebacking in, you'll likely have definite weight and space limitations to observe. Again, your outfitter should provide this information.

Commercial airline baggage handlers are notoriously tough on firearms, which must be sturdily cased before being shipped. Soft vinyl or leather zipper cases aren't suitable protection. Hard plastic luggage-type cases offer a certain degree of protection but seldom hold up for more than one or two flights. The best bet for sending fine rifles or shotguns by air is one of the excellent foam-padded, all-aluminum firearms cases on the market. These are expensive, but they're cheap insurance against firearm or riflescope damage. These cases should be locked, and a few wrappings with

fiberglass-filament shipping tape adds extra security en route. Incidentally, all firearms shipped as airline baggage must be unloaded and there should be no loose ammunition in the container. You'll be asked to sign a statement to that effect when you check the gun case through, and you'll be held legally responsible if the gun should happen to fire while the case is being handled as baggage. That's admittedly a rare occurrence, but it *has* happened—which is why airlines are now so strict about the rule. The ticket agent may also ask you to open the case so that he can inspect the firearm.

Anytime you transport a scoped rifle any distance, whether it's in an airplane or the truck of your car, you should always re-check the rifle's zero when you arrive at your destination. It's always possible for the scope or its mounts to be jarred enough to cause you to miss what you're shooting at. Always plan to spend a few minutes shooting at a paper target,

Anytime you transport a scoped rifle any distance, you should always recheck its zero before you begin hunting.

with the rifle supported by sandbags or some other suitable rest (a rolled-up sleeping bag or jacket will do) when you arrive in camp. Bring some extra ammo along for this purpose, as it may take several shots to get the sights in proper adjustment again.

Hiring an Outfitter

If you elect to hire an outfitter or guide to help you find game in some unfamiliar locale, you'll need to begin a year or more in advance. Once you've decided on where—and what—you want to hunt, you must then choose the guide that will do you a good job. As in any business, there are both good and bad guides and outfitters. The trick is to tell them apart *before* you've paid your money and wasted a couple of weeks on a bad hunt.

How do you choose a guide? Most hunters check the outfitters' ads in the back of the national hunting and outdoor magazines. The National Rifle Association (1600 Rhode Island Ave. NW, Washington, DC 20036) publishes

an annual *Denali Guide* that lists many outfitters, or you can write the game and fish department of the state or province you intend to hunt in for a list of licensed guides.

Once you have a likely list of prospects, send a personal letter to at least a half dozen, if possible. Ask for the outfitter's brochure, if he has one. Find out what areas he conducts hunts in, and when. Ask what hunting dates are still open for the following season. Check to see if he hunts from a permanent base camp or lodge, or from distant spike camps. Hunting from a lodge offers greater comfort, but spike camp forays are more likely to produce trophy game.

Certainly ask about price, and find out how much deposit is required to reserve a hunting date. Find out, too, about the possibility of a partial refund, and how much, if you're for some reason forced to cancel out after you've signed on. Be sure to find out if you'll be paired with other hunters, or if each client will have his or her own guide during the hunt. One-on-one hunts are costly, and you're likely to get a better rate if you hunt with a friend and share a guide between you. Ask about this possibility.

Finally—and perhaps most important—ask the outfitter/guide for a reference list of ex-customers. Then write or call four or five of these references and ask for a candid appraisal of the outfitter and his services. The guide isn't likely to list anyone he *knows* is disgruntled with him, but a few telephone conversations with past clients can be highly revealing. The money and time you spend on this kind of detective work will be well spent if it helps you avoid paying several thousand dollars for a bad hunt.

If you know anyone who hunts regularly in the area you hope to hunt in, ask *him* to recommend an outfitter. If someone you're acquainted with honestly recommends a guide he's had experience with, chances are that guide will be a safe choice.

Before you make your final decision and write that deposit check, give the prospective outfitter a telephone call and talk things over.

The best campsites are on high ground, away from tall grass and heavy brush.

Backpack hunts place a premium on weight, space, and advance planning. With packbag removed, pack frames can be used for carrying out game. This hunter is carrying venison on Coleman's Peak 1 flexible pack frame.

There's no substitute for personal conversation when it comes to making this kind of choice. This is the chance to ask those questions you've overlooked in your earlier correspondence. If you're not satisfied with the answers, try the next guide on your list.

Plan for Physical Stress

Whenever you plan a guided hunt, you know you're going to be riding and/or hiking in some rugged, wild country, possibly several thousand feet above sea level. This means you should begin some kind of regular exercise program several months in advance to get you in shape. It's wise to check with your doctor first, and ask him to recommend a suitable regimen. Even active sportsmen are likely to find mountain hunting surprisingly rigorous, and sedentary types may find themselves all but helpless if they fail to get into the proper physical condition first.

Choosing a Campsite

If you and your party will be hunting on your own, your planning isn't done until you've arrived and selected a safe campsite. Observe the following checklist:

· Don't camp under dead snags or tall trees that may attract lightning. Wind, snow, or rain may cause limbs or dead trees to fall on you as you sleep. These snags and trees are called "widowmakers," for obvious reasons.

· Don't camp in tall grass or near heavy brush during dry weather when the fire hazards are high. Avoid camping near swamps, as they breed mosquitoes and other pesky insects that can make your life miserable.

· Never take it for granted that lake or stream water is pure. It's safer to boil the water, or treat it with purification tablets before drinking.

· Never pitch camp in a gully or canyon where a sudden flash flood several miles away might wash you and your gear away. If you camp or hunt in a coastal area, pitch your camp well above the high tide mark. And keep an eye on the tide to make sure you don't find yourself stranded several hours at a time.

· Never camp under an overhanging cliff or bluff where rock slides or avalanches may endanger you or your camp. The best campsite is on high ground, away from beach, lake, or stream where it will be protected from high winds, but where it will receive some cooling breezes to keep insects away.

· Pitch your tent on a level knoll or slight slope so that the ground provides natural drainage. Try to keep clear of marshy soils or clay where mud and rain may collect. The tent should be erected so that the entrance isn't pointed directly into the prevailing wind. A southeast-facing tent will be warmed faster by the morning sun, but wind direction should be the deciding factor. Use a separate tarp over the tent whenever possible for maximum protection in nasty weather.

Backpack Hunts

Backpack hunts have their own peculiar planning problems, as weight and space have a high premium. Generally speaking, you shouldn't try to carry more than a third of your weight, and most sportsmen are happier with a much smaller burden. A good backpack that *fits* you is of utmost importance. It should be designed with a waist support to place most of the pack's weight on your hips.

Lightweight tents and down- or synthetic-filled sleeping bags are needed for backpacking, and freeze-dried or dehydrated foods are required to keep weight down. Lightweight rifles are also a fine idea. Most sportsmen who decide to combine hunting with backpacking already have a pretty good idea of what backpacking is about, and know how to buy and pack their provisions and equipment. If this kind of superlight going is new to you, *The Hiker's Bible* or some other good backpacking book is recommended reading before you attempt your first backpacking hunt.

Every hunt requires a certain amount of advance planning, even if it's only to make sure you have your alarm set to ring at the proper time in the morning, and check to see that your gun and ammunition are close at hand. You also need to know exactly where you're going the next morning, and you should tell someone when you plan to return. The simplest hunting trip makes certain demands of the planning process. Forget a vital item—like ammunition or your hunting license—and the entire trip may be ruined.

Trips that take several days or weeks and involve distant travel are much more complicated and require more detailed planning. But planning is anticipation and can be nearly as much fun as the hunting trip itself. Don't begrudge the time you spend making plans. If you've thought carefully ahead and are properly prepared, you'll be able to relax and have a wonderful hunt.

3

Which Firearm—Rifle, Shotgun, or Handgun?

There are three basic types of firearms available for hunting: rifles, handguns, and shotguns. Rifles and shotguns both have long barrels, and are supported against the shoulder during shooting. The chief difference between them is that the rifle shoots a single projectile, or bullet, and is designed to allow reasonably precise placement of that bullet out to 200 or 300 yards. Shotguns throw several hundred tiny pellets in an expanding pattern and have a maximum effective range of around 50 yards.

Like rifles, handguns are designed to shoot one bullet at a time. However, they're much more compact and lack a shoulder stock. They're held at arm's length and grasped in one or both of the shooter's hands. With the proper marksmanship, a handgun suitable for hunting will kill game at a greater range than a shotgun, though not as far away as a rifle.

Choosing a Firearm

Rifles and handguns are used to hunt both large and small game but never to hunt waterfowl or upland game birds. The only kind of bird regularly hunted with rifles is the wild turkey.

Conversely, shotguns are used to hunt almost every kind of game. It's the only firearm really useful for shooting flying or fast-moving game, and many sportsmen regard the shotgun as a bird gun only. But in some parts of the country, heavy buckshot- or slug-loaded shotguns are popular among deer hunters. As a matter of fact, the shotgun is the only legal hunting firearm in certain heavily populated areas where a far-ranging rifle bullet might be dangerous.

Both rifles and handguns are used to hunt deer and other game. The Ruger autoloading carbine (LEFT) and Ruger Super Blackhawk revolver (RIGHT) are both chambered for the .44 magnum cartridge and are suitable for hunting deer.

Neither handgun nor shotgun is intended for long-range hunting. A flat-shooting rifle can kill beyond 400 yards in the hands of an expert.

Rabbit and squirrel hunters use all three firearm types. Their rifles and handguns are more likely to shoot rimfire .22s than the more powerful centerfire cartridges used by deer hunters. When .22 rimfires are used, sportsmen try to very carefully place each shot to ensure clean kills. Most shooting is done well this side of the 75-yard mark, as the little 40-grain .22-caliber projectile lacks sufficient energy to do the job at much longer distances. The small-game rifleman also waits until his target is stationary. It's possible to hit a moving mark with a rifle, but it takes a fair amount of skill and practice.

If running game is expected, shotguns are normally called for. The wide, spreading shot pattern from an open-choked scattergun allows a wider margin of error and greatly improves your chances for scoring. Also, shotguns are pointed, *not* precisely aimed. You don't have to carefully align the sights on target and then s-q-u-e-e-z-e the trigger. Many experienced scattergunners aren't even aware of seeing the barrel as they swing on a passing bird and slap the trigger. Shotguns are designed for speedy, instinctive shooting; rifles are intended for precise, steady marksmanship.

Not too many years ago, it was illegal to hunt deer and other large game with a handgun in many states. As sport handgunning has gained in popularity, those laws have been changed and certain specified handgun cartridges can now be used to legally hunt deer in most parts of the country. That attitude isn't universal, though, so be sure to check your own state game laws before you decide to seek this season's trophy with a six-gun in your hand. Keep in mind that only a few magnum cartridges are considered adequate for deer-sized game. These typically include the .357, .41, and .44 magnums, as well as a few of the more powerful wildcat or rifle chamberings available in some of the single-shot pistols on the market.

Generally speaking, the handgun should only be used by experts when it comes to hunting game. It requires expert stalking skills to sneak within handgun range of a skittish buck,

Rabbit and squirrel hunters are likely to shoot .22 rimfire rifles, which are effective to about 75 yards.

Handguns should only be used by experts for hunting game. It takes both stalking and shooting skill to bag game with a handgun.

Shotguns are used to hit fast-moving game like these western sage grouse.

If you intend to hunt flying game, you'll need a shotgun.

and an even higher level of marksmanship to get the job done right. Handguns take a lot more time and patience to master than rifles do. Another consideration is the fact that it's very difficult to legally own a handgun in some parts of the country. If you live in a community where handgun ownership is rigorously discouraged by local lawmakers, you're likely better off doing your hunting with a shotgun or rifle.

Most hunters use both rifles and shotguns, while an increasing number of sportsmen also own and hunt with handguns. As already noted, it's impossible to hunt flying game safely and effectively with a rifle or a revolver. If you intend to hunt ducks or geese, or pheasant and quail, you'll need a shotgun; some wingshooters own a whole battery of scat-

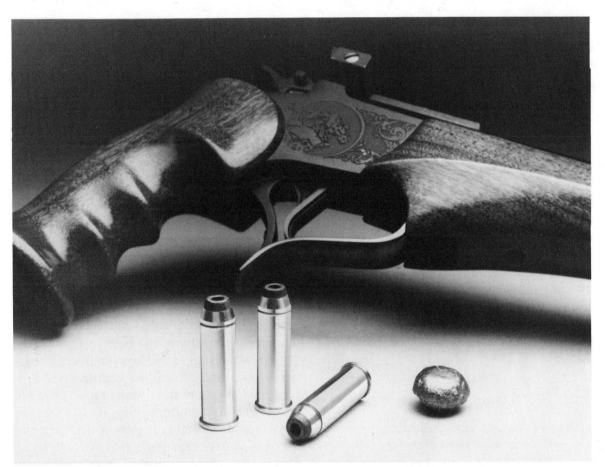

Only a few magnum handgun cartridges are adequate for deer-sized game. The .41 Remington Magnum cartridge, for which this Thompson/Center Contender pistol is chambered, is a good choice.

terguns, each intended for a different type of game. Shotgun barrels are choked differently to throw shot pellets in a dense, tightly clustered cloud for downing targets 40 or even 50 yards from the muzzle, or in a loose, wide pattern for birds flushed at close range. Shotgun gauges and barrel lengths also differ, and each gauge/barrel length/choke combination has its own application.

The majority of riflemen these days depend on magnifying glass sights, or "scopes," in the hunting field. These optical sighting aids not only magnify and clarify the target image, but also allow safe shooting both earlier and later in the day. Twilight targets that are shadowed and indistinct when viewed over open iron sights stand out clearly when seen through a 4-power scope.

Even handgunners are turning to scopes, particularly when armed with one of the modern, flat-shooting single shot pistols now available. Magnum revolver fans are also mounting handgun scopes on their guns. Scopes designed for handgun use are typically of low magnification—1½ or 2X—and allow the scope to be held at arm's length. Rifle scopes have more critical eye relief, and must be held no farther than 4 or 5 inches from the shooter's eye to allow proper viewing.

Muzzle-loading rifles and shotguns firing hand-poured charges of old-fashioned black powder or Pyrodex, its modern counterpart, are used to hunt all kinds of game. Separate hunting seasons are often set aside for black powder riflemen. Black-powder-shooting pistols aren't potent enough for anything but small game. Using any muzzle-loading firearm reduces a hunter's effective shooting range and offers a greater challenge than modern firearms do.

Taking Care of Your Firearms

Rifles, handguns, and shotguns are built to last a lifetime with proper care and maintenance. New guns should be gone over carefully and all grease or spray preservatives in which they may be packed when shipped should be

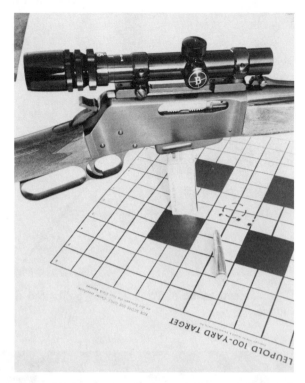

Most riflemen depend on magnifying-glass sights. This .358 Winchester Browning lever rifle mounts a Bushnell Scopechief 1½–4½X variable model.

removed. Firing a weapon with heavy gun grease in the barrel can result in a serious accident not only to the gun, but also to the shooter. If you accidentally drop your gun in dirt or snow, be sure none of it has plugged the barrel—wipe the gun off and *don't fire it* until you are sure the bore is clear. If you are hunting in extremely cold weather, oil and grease can stiffen and slow down the action of the firing pin to the point where it does not strike the cartridge primer with sufficient force to fire it. Use a gun solvent and remove all oil.

When hunting in the foggy and wet coastal areas near salt water, the firearm should be wiped off now and then during the day with an oily cloth to prevent rusting. When through with the day's hunt, it pays to run powder-solvent-soaked cleaning patches through the bore. Repeat the process, now using dry patches. When these come through clean, run through a patch soaked with a light grade of gun oil. Use a soft oily cloth to wipe out the action and all outside metal parts so that all moisture and perspiration from your hands are removed.

Storing Arms

Before you store your firearms for several months, they should be thoroughly cleaned and oiled. If stored for longer periods, they should be given a light coat of gun grease, or a preservative should be sprayed on them. Never plug up the barrel or leave an oily rag or cord in it. Beware of some sheepskin-lined gun boots and cases. These can cause a gun to sweat, and the material may contain tanning chemicals or dye that will cause rust and ruin the gun finish.

4

The Hunting Rifle

Various kinds of rifles are used for hunting different kinds of game. Rabbit and squirrel hunters use lightweight firearms chambered for inexpensive .22 rimfire ammunition, while sportsmen who shoot ground squirrels and woodchucks several hundred yards away employ much heavier, bull-barreled varmint rifles firing high-velocity .22 centerfire cartridges.

Deer hunters use everything from light, handy .30-30 saddle carbines to bolt-action magnums fitted with high-magnification scope sights. Hunters of larger game like moose and elk favor more powerful rifles than the average deer hunter requires, while sportsmen who tackle big, dangerous game like Alaskan brown bear demand booming big-bores with enough oomph to stop a close-range charge.

Choosing the Right Cartridge

A large variety of rifle cartridges are available to suit nearly every hunting situation.

Cottontails and jackrabbits are fairly easy to kill, and the light report and low recoil of the .22 long rifle rimfire round make it very pleasant to shoot. Since the .22 long rifle is both accurate and powerful enough to kill small game cleanly out to 75 yards or so, it's little wonder rifles chambered for this cartridge are so overwhelmingly popular.

Moving up to the .22 magnum rimfire lets you stretch your rifle range to 125 yards or a bit more. This round is more than twice as costly as its smaller rimfire cousin, but it's still considerably less expensive than buying .22 centerfire factory loads.

While these two rimfires make fine choices for hunting small game, they offer limited range and lack the power necessary for hunting deer.

Medium- to long-range varmint hunters have several suitable cartridges to choose from. These include all the popular .22 centerfires from the .22 Hornet to the .22-250 Remington

Rimfire .22s are popular among squirrel and rabbit hunters. These soft-spoken rifles have almost non-existent recoil, and are effective to 75 yards or so.

and .220 Swift. A few varminters use the Lilliputian .17 Remington or develop their own "wildcat" rounds. These .22 and smaller-caliber cartridges are varmint loads, pure and simple. Some centerfire .22s have been used to hunt deer successfully, but they're not really suited to taking deer or larger game. Some states specifically outlaw the use of any .22-caliber rifle, rimfire or centerfire, in the deer woods.

Sportsmen who would like to use the same rifle for hunting both varmints and deer-sized game have a number of excellent cartridges that will do the job. Winchester's .243 or Remington's 6mm rounds make fine deer-hunting medicine when loaded with 100-grain (or heavier) bullets; when it's time to shoot varmints, simply switch to lighter 80- or 90-grain

loads. The .250 Savage, .257 Roberts, and .25-06 Remington also fit the combination deer/varmint cartridge category. None of these rounds develops excessive recoil, although the .25-06 Remington produces a noticeable jolt.

The .25 calibers and 6mm (the .243 Winchester is really a 6mm) rounds just named also make fine cartridges for those who hunt only deer and antelope. With their heaviest bullet weights, they shoot flat enough and hard enough to kill such animals out to 250 yards, and without a lot of unpleasant recoil. The .25-06 is effective out to 350 yards or more on deer-sized game, provided the bullet is properly placed.

The great middle ground of deer cartridges includes the .270 Winchester, 7mm Mauser, 7mm/08 Remington, 7mm Express Remington

These 7mm rounds belong to the great "middle ground" of deer cartridges. The 7mm Remington Magnum (FAR LEFT) is the most potent, while the 7mm-08 Remington (RIGHT) is designed for short-action rifles. All are fine choices for deer-sized game.

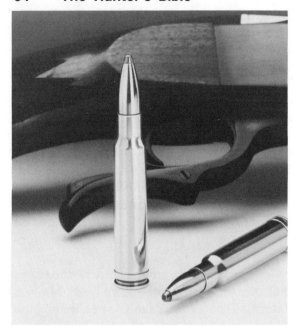

The .338 Winchester Magnum is a big-bore caliber for large game like elk or moose and is potent enough for Alaska's giant grizzlies. (FEDERAL CARTRIDGE PHOTO)

(also known as the .280 Remington), .308 Winchester, .307 Winchester, and the .30-06. All of these cartridges are adequately powered for both deer and larger game like elk, and have an effective range well beyond 300 yards. They all develop only moderate recoil, yet shoot flat enough to hit the vitals of a deer-sized animal out to 275 yards without requiring much sighting holdover (assuming the rifle has been properly zeroed to put the bullet 2½ or 3 inches above the line of sight at 100 yards). Any of these choices are outstanding deer rounds and do a fine job at both short and long range.

Some hunters prefer the light handiness of one of the lever-action carbines offered by U.S. Repeating Arms, Marlin, and other manufacturers and buy these firearms chambered for the .30-30 Winchester, .35 Remington, or .44 magnum cartridges. These are all good woods rounds but their looping trajectories make them poor choices for ranges much farther than 100 yards. The .30-30 is nearly a century old and is outmoded by most modern ballistic standards. At the same time, more deer have

undoubtedly fallen to the .30-30 than to any other cartridge. Within its range limitations, its effectiveness on deer has been too often proven to remain open to question. At the same time, the .307 and .356 Winchester lever carbine loads now available are more potent and versatile.

For that matter, both Browning and Savage make lever-action rifles chambered for such modern deer loads as the .243 Winchester, the 7mm-08 Remington, and the .308 Winchester. Even larger calibers like the .358 Winchester, .444 Marlin, and .45-70 are available in lever-action chamberings. These generate more recoil, but are potent enough for moose, as well as deer-sized game.

When it comes to hunting moose and elk, most of the "middle ground" deer cartridges mentioned are adequate, but many hunters feel more comfortable having even greater power at hand. The 7mm and .300 belted magnums are top choices here; they offer power to spare for even long-range kills. They do recoil harder than lesser rounds, but not hard enough to discourage many deer hunters from carrying rifles chambered for these potent numbers.

Remington's 8mm magnum and the .338 Winchester magnum are also used on elk and moose, and offer enough power for hunting brown bears and mountain grizzlies. The .375 Holland & Holland magnum makes a great charge stopper if a disgruntled Alaskan bruin takes a sudden dislike to you, but it offers more power than is really needed for any other North American game. The .375 H&H and the other big-bore magnums just mentioned sport fairly lusty recoil, though you're not likely to notice it when viewing a grizzly through your sights.

Rifle Types

There are five basic rifle types available: pump, autoloader, lever action, bolt action, and single shot. Autoloaders and pumps offer fast follow-up shots, and the autoloading action softens apparent recoil. However, these fast-repeating actions can be fussy about the

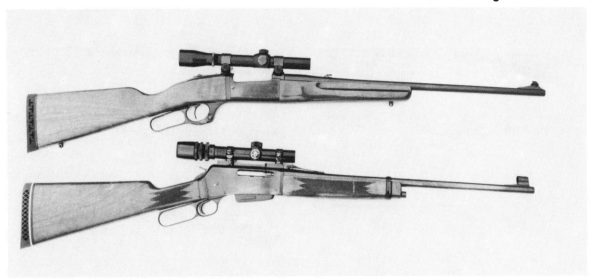

Both Savage (TOP) and Browning (BOTTOM) make lever-action rifles potent enough for nearly all North American large game.

Autoloaders like this .30-06 Remington offer reduced recoil, rapid repeat shots, but can be fussy about reloaded ammunition.

Lever rifles are traditional in some parts of the country; some hunters will use no other type.

kind of ammunition they're fed, particularly when reloads are used. Also, they're seldom capable of the ultra-fine accuracy some bolt rifles will often deliver. They're plenty accurate for hunting deer and other large game but lack the real tack-driving ability long-range varmint hunters need.

Nearly all varmint rifles are of the bolt-action variety, primarily because bolt rifles are consistently the best performers in the accuracy department. When you're shooting at a target no more than 2 or 3 inches square at a distance of 200 or even 300 yards, you need a rifle that's capable of grouping its shots inside a circle no more than an inch across from 100 yards. A rifle that will do this is said to deliver minute-of-angle accuracy.

Bolt rifles are favored by many deer and big-

Browning BBR Lightning Bolt

Remington Model 700

Ruger M-77

Remington Model 788

game hunters for other reasons, too. The turn-bolt action is very strong and offers plenty of camming power to extract recalcitrant cartridge cases from the chamber. It's the most reliable of the repeaters and can be depended on to keep operating under conditions that might put other action types out of order. Because of its strength, it can be chambered for the most powerful hunting cartridges on the market.

There are several lightweight bolt rifles you can buy that are beautifully balanced, easy to carry, and very accurate. Remington, Ruger, Winchester, Browning, and others all manufacture featherweight bolt-action firearms in a variety of useful chamberings. By way of contrast, most of these manufacturers also make bull-barreled, heavyweight bolt rifles for the varmint-shooting set.

Lever rifles are traditional in many parts of the country, and some hunters will use no other type. Lever-action firearms offer fairly fast follow-up shots, and some are capable of surprising accuracy. The lightweight saddle carbines sold in .30-30 and similar calibers owe their long-standing popularity more to their light weight, compact size, and easy handling than to the cartridges they digest.

Single-shot hunting rifles appeal to the rifle-

Bolt-action rifles like this Model 70 Winchester are strong and reliable. These rifles are available in almost all popular calibers.

man who prides himself on his ability to get the job done with the single round at his disposal. Actually, sportsmen who use single shots aren't handicapping themselves all that much. The fact is, your best chance to anchor game in its tracks is with that first shot. If that shot misses, your follow-up attempts will likely be made at a frantically running or bounding animal. One shot heard in the deer woods usually signifies success; a hurried barrage means it's three to one the deer was missed and made its escape.

Because single-shot rifles have no reciprocating action to add to their length, they're typically shorter than a bolt rifle sporting a barrel of the same length. This means you can have a single shot sporting a 26-inch barrel without exceeding the overall length of a bolt make sure the bullet goes where you intended. Lever carbines and other short, fast-handling rifles intended for close-range hunting are often used with the open iron sights installed by the factory as standard equipment. These sights are satisfactory out to 100 yards or so but are too coarse for precise bullet placement at much longer range.

Most modern nimrods depend on some kind of magnifying scope sight and have these sights installed on or soon after purchase of a new hunting rifle. Bushnell, Bausch & Lomb, Burris, Leupold, Redfield, Tasco, Nikon, and others all offer excellent medium-priced sights, while several premium-priced, and premium-quality, sights are imported from West Germany and Austria. Scopes meant for hunting should be fogproof and waterproof and should be capable of withstanding the shock of repeated recoil. Don't make the mistake of buying the cheapest economy scope you can find. Buy the best you can afford, since this isn't the place to economize. A scope that leaks, fogs, or fails to hold its zero can ruin an expensive and time-consuming hunt.

In addition to magnifying the target, a good scope offers a brighter, greatly clarified viewing image. This allows you to lengthen your shooting day, as you can see your target clearly 10 or 15 minutes earlier in the morning, and later in the afternoon. Scopes are also a great boon to riflemen with failing eyesight.

Scopes are available in several magnifications. The most useful models for hunting deer and other game offer magnification in the 2X to 8X or 9X range. Greater magnification isn't needed, and is actually detrimental. The greater the magnification, the smaller the viewing field. A 4X model may provide a field of view measuring 36 feet across at 100 yards, while 6X magnification reduces that to 23 feet. A 10X scope cuts your view to a tunnel just 12 feet wide. The greater the viewing field, the less trouble you'll have finding the animal in the scope reticle. This translates directly into aiming speed. A low magnification scope may not enlarge the target several times, but will be much faster to use than a high-powered model.

Because they lack a reciprocating action, single-shot rifles are shorter and more compact than most repeaters. The Ruger No. 1 International carbine at right is substantially shorter than the Sako bolt rifle, left.

rifle wearing a shorter 22-inch tube. The longer barrel typically generates between 100 and 150 feet per second (fps) greater bullet velocity, which means better performance.

Choosing a Rifle Sight

Regardless of which action type you prefer, you'll need some kind of sighting equipment to

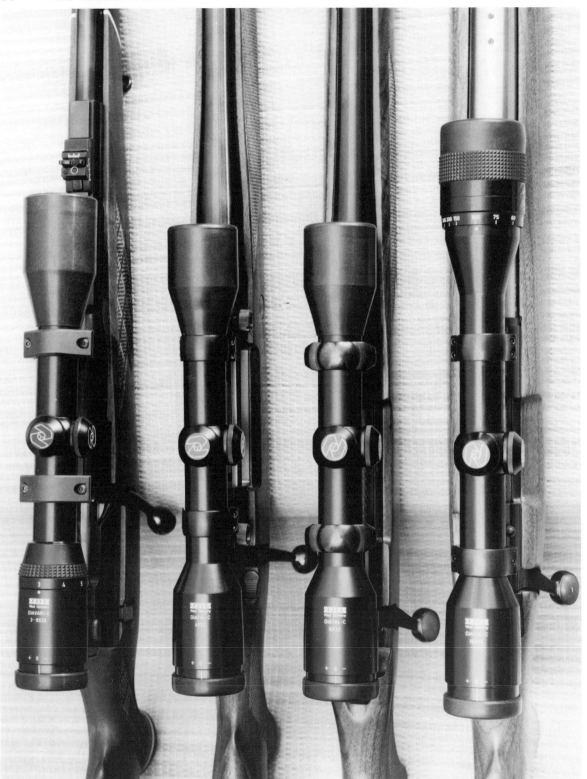

Riflescopes are the most popular kind of rifle sights for hunting. This Zeiss lineup shows (FROM LEFT) 3-9X variable model, and fixed-power 4X, 6X, and 10X sights.

For many years, the fixed-power 4X scope was the overwhelming favorite of deer and big game hunters alike. It's still a fine choice. Fixed-power scopes are less expensive and at least theoretically less fragile than variable-magnification models. However, the ability to zoom from 3X to 9X with a twist of the tube is seductive, and the 3–9X variable is the largest selling model now available. This 3–9X power combination is most useful on dual-duty rifles that will be used for hunting deer and small varmints alike. Set on 3X magnification, such a scope offers a fast, clear sight picture that's useful on both standing or running game; cranked up to 9X, it magnifies sufficiently to turn tiny rodents into reasonable targets.

While most 3–9X variables are bulky, there are smaller 2–7X and even 1½–4½X models available. These offer more than enough magnification for the average deer and elk hunter. The 1½–4½X glasses are the number one choice of hunters of large, dangerous game; at 1½X, these sights can be used with both eyes open, and are very fast.

Heavy-barreled varmint rifles often mount large 10X and 12X sights, and there are 4–12X and 6–18X variable models available for this specialized brand of shooting.

There are several different scopes on the market with range-finding reticles. These typically feature a pair of stadia cross hairs that can be moved closer together or farther apart by turning an adjustment dial. A deer or similar-size animal measures an average of 18 inches from the top of his shoulders to the bottom of his brisket. The range-finding scopes make use of this supposition. The stadia hairs are adjusted so that they just bracket the animal's chest cavity, and then the rifleman can read the computed distance to the target on a range dial provided. He can then either raise the cross hairs sufficiently above the intended target to allow for bullet drop at that range, or simply turn another dial to make this adjustment automatically. Then if the animal is still patiently waiting around, the sportsman shoots.

A less complicated and in many ways more

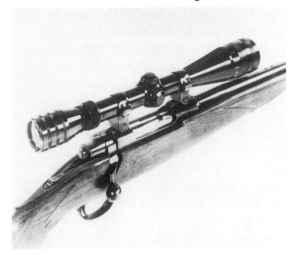

Varmint rifles often mount high-magnification sights like the 10X Redfield shown on this Ruger M-77V bolt rifle.

practical approach to long-range hunting marksmanship is to adjust the sights so that the bullets impact 2½ to 3 inches above point of aim at the 100-yard mark. With most of the modern, flat-shooting deer and big game cartridges recommended, you can then hold dead on target out to 250 or 275 yards without worrying too much about bullet drop. The bullet will rise 2 or 3 inches above point of aim at short range, and fall a maximum of maybe 5 or 6 inches at 275 yards. That means you *won't* miss the vital area of a deer-sized target because you failed to compensate for the bullet's trajectory. You can still *miss,* but it won't be the fault of ballistics.

Rifle sights should be checked before every hunting season to make sure they haven't shifted. You use the same procedure to sight in a newly mounted riflescope. If possible, have the scope boresighted immediately after it's mounted. This should be done before the scoped rifle leaves the store or the gunsmith's shop. Boresighting simply means that your first shot fired at a target 25 yards (paces) away *should* print somewhere on the target paper. A boresighted rifle is *not* ready for the hunting field.

Take the scoped rifle to the nearest rifle

range, along with a supply of the same kind of ammunition you'll be using on the hunt. It's a mistake to economize by using war surplus or some other ammo for sighting in, and then switching to another type for hunting. Brand, load, and bullet weight all have their effect on where the bullet strikes in relation to the sight picture. Use only the exact type—brand, load, bullet style, and bullet weight—you intend to hunt with.

If a shooting bench is available, place the rifle on sandbags or some other kind of firm, yet yielding support. Otherwise, use a rolled-up sleeping bag or jacket as a rest and shoot from a steady prone position or across the hood of your car. It's important to keep that rifle perfectly steady to eliminate as much human error as possible during the sighting-in process.

Next, place a printed target—or a large piece of white paper with a small bull's-eye drawn in its center—on a cardboard box and set the box 25 yards downrange. Return to your rifle, hold it perfectly steady against whatever rest you've devised, center the bull's-eye in the cross hairs, take a deep breath, let it partway out, and carefully s-q-u-e-e-z-e the trigger.

Check the target to see where the bullet struck. If it was 2 inches low and 3 inches to the left, you must move the cross hairs to compensate. The adjustment dials are found at the center of most riflescope tubes, and wear screw-on covers. The vertical dial makes changes in elevation, while the dial oriented horizontally lets you move the cross hairs left and right for needed windage adjustments.

Move the cross hairs in the same direction

Rifles should be sighted in using the same kind of ammunition that will be used to hunt with. Rifle should be solidly supported by a sandbagged rest to reduce human error.

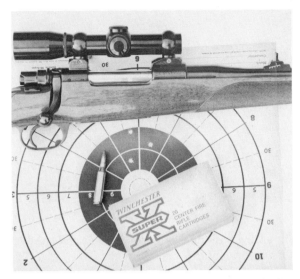

Most popular hunting calibers sighted in to print 2½ or 3 inches high at 100 yards will let you hold "dead on" out to 275 yards when shooting deer-sized game.

you want the bullet strike to move. This means you need to raise the point of impact 2 inches, and move it 3 inches to the right. Each increment or click of the adjusting screw will move the bullet strike ¼ or ½ inch at a range of 100 yards. When you shoot at 25 yards, you must dial in 4 times that adjustment. With ½-inch clicks at 100 yards, moving the bullet strike up 2 inches would require 4 clicks. At 25 yards, that same adjustment requires 4×4, or 16 clicks.

Shoot at the same target again. When the bullet strike is within an inch of the bull's-eye center (or whatever aiming mark you're using), move the target until it's 100 yards away from the firing point. Then begin the same procedure over once again. You shoot at 25 yards first to make sure the sights are adjusted well enough to have the bullet at least print on paper at 100 yards. As mentioned earlier, zeroing your rifle in so that the bullet strikes 2½ or 3 inches directly above the bull's-eye from the 100-yard range will allow you to hold "dead on" a deer-sized animal out to 275 yards without compensating for the bullet's curving flight.

When shooting from a solid rest, you should be able to put three consecutive shots into a group measuring no more than 2½ or 3 inches across—and preferably less. That's adequate deer woods accuracy, but it isn't precise enough for long-range varmint shooting at small rodents. For this kind of sport, the group size should be an inch or less. If you're getting poorer performance, try tightening the rifle's guard screws. Then check the scope and mounts to make sure everything's tight and secure. Finally, you might try a different brand of ammunition or a different bullet weight. If you handload, try a slightly lighter or heavier (if safe) load. A lot of variables can affect rifle accuracy—sometimes changing just one of these variables makes a big difference in group size.

Rifle Shooting Positions

Once you have your rifle properly sighted in with the same ammunition you'll be using to hunt with, you should practice until you can shoot it confidently. There are four basic shooting positions riflemen use in the hunting field. The first is the standing or offhand position. This is the basic rifleman's stance, as it's the easiest and fastest one to assume. Unfortunately, it's also the least steady and should only be used for shooting game at relatively close range, or when there's no chance to drop into one of the more stable positions. To shoot a rifle offhand, stand with the body facing about 90 degrees to the right of the target (reverse this direction if you're left-handed). Spread the feet a comfortable distance apart, with your weight evenly distributed between them. Cradle the fore-end of your rifle in your left palm, and grasp the pistol grip in your right hand (again, unless you're a southpaw). Raise the rifle to shooting position and pull the butt snugly against your right shoulder. The right arm should be roughly parallel with the ground, while the left elbow should be directly under the rifle for maximum support. Your cheek should rest on the stock's comb or cheekpiece. Remember to squeeze—not pull—

The sitting position is both comfortable and steady; it's a favorite of experienced hunters.

The standing, or offhand, position is the least steady but the fastest and easiest stance to assume. It's fine for close or running game but should be avoided for long-range shooting.

Whenever possible, take advantage of tree trunks, boulders, and other natural rests to steady your aim, but don't allow the rifle to come in direct contact with such hard, unyielding surfaces. Cushion it with your hands or with a rolled-up jacket.

the trigger when the sights are steady on the mark you're shooting at.

The kneeling position is a bit steadier. Right-handed riflemen should kneel on their right knee, and lean forward until the left elbow rests just ahead of the upthrust left kneecap. Again, the bent right arm should be parallel with the ground, and the left elbow should be directly under the rifle's barrel.

The sitting position is steadier yet and is more comfortable than the kneeling position. An experienced shooter can drop into the sitting position in about the same length of time it takes to assume the kneeling stance.

Simply sit down, facing at a shallow angle to the right of the target, with your legs well apart. Bend the knees. Holding the rifle to your shoulder in shooting position, lean forward and rest both elbows just ahead of the kneecaps (resting them directly on the kneecaps provides a wobblier rest). The right arm should be slightly inside the right leg, and supported just below the knee. The sitting position is a favorite of hunters, as it positions the rifle high enough to let you see over high grass or brush and offers good support.

The prone position is the steadiest for long-range work, but you may have trouble seeing over the surrounding brush. It can also be awkward for sharply angled uphill shots. To assume the prone position, lie on your stomach with your body angled 30 to 45 degrees to the right of the target. Spread the legs a comfortable distance, with the heels turned inward. Place the left elbow directly under the rifle and cradle the fore-end in the left palm. Place the right arm and elbow at a comfortable angle. Both elbows should be on the ground.

While those are the basic rifle-shooting positions, you can hold your rifle even steadier if you take advantage of natural rests in the field. Boulders, tree trunks, fence posts, and stumps all offer excellent support, and the smart hunter takes full advantage of them. Placing your backpack or a rolled-up jacket on the ground also provides a good field rest. Don't rest the rifle stock directly against any hard, unyielding object, though, as this may jar the barrel under recoil and throw the bullet several feet off course. Instead, place your hand, a glove, a folded jacket, or any other cushioning material between stock and rest.

Don't get the idea that it's not sporting to shoot from a rest; the true sportsman does everything possible to ensure accurate bullet placement when hunting game. A properly placed bullet means a quick, clean kill, while a badly placed shot may only wound the animal. For the same reason, experienced riflemen are the ones least likely to attempt a shot when the game is out of range. Three hundred yards is a l-o-n-g shot for the average rifleman. If at all possible, it's better to try stalking closer than to shoot at extended ranges. The closer you get, the better your chances of connecting.

Your Target

That brings up another point. An experienced rifleman never shoots at an animal—he shoots at a particular *spot* on that animal. For most game like deer and elk, shooting for the shoulder or at a spot immediately behind the shoulder is your best bet. A bullet here will pierce the shoulder and/or the lungs, and if the shot goes low it's likely to shatter the heart. Aim at the rear portion of the shoulder about midway up on the animal's body. A shot that goes high should hit the spine. Some deer hunters like to shoot for the neck; this is a much smaller mark but can be instantly fatal if you connect.

If the animal is traveling toward you, hitting almost anywhere along the vertical line from its nose to its brisket will be effective. If the only target offered is of the animal moving directly away, hitting anywhere along the spine will anchor it.

Needless to say, a running animal is much harder to hit than a stationary one, and running shots should be avoided, if possible. If you *must* shoot at an animal running broadside, you must swing the sights ahead and continue to maintain that lead as you pull the trigger. Determining the amount of lead necessary requires a fair amount of experience and practice. The lead can be measured in several feet or inches, depending on how far away the animal is and how fast he's moving. An animal angling toward you or away requires less lead than one running at a right angle to the line of fire. The only sure thing you know is that if you *fail* to lead a running animal, you'll miss.

5

The Hunting Shotgun

Shotguns are designed to hit moving targets at close range. They throw hundreds of tiny shot pellets in a spreading pattern, so precise marksmanship isn't necessary. Consequently, shotguns are quickly pointed, *not* carefully aimed.

Rather than rely on rifle-type sights, the shotgunner points at game instinctively. He may be conscious of the single round bead at the muzzle, but the way he moves his body with the gun is more important than the rudimentary sighting equipment provided. Gun fit is therefore more important than it is to a rifleman.

The majority of mass-produced shotguns available today all feature more-or-less standard stock dimensions. And the average shooter is able to adapt pretty well to the way a standard stock fits him. But if the gun is noticeably too long from trigger to buttplate, too

short, or has a comb that's too high, too thick, too thin, or too low, the shooter will have a hard time scoring well with it. This means a very large or very small gunner, or a shooter with extra short or extra long arms may have to alter the stock to suit him.

Fortunately, most shooters are able to do very well with standard production shotgun stocks. Competitive trap and skeet shooters are very fussy about the way their guns fit them, but the average duck and pheasant hunter pays little attention to fit. If the gun feels right when he or she throws the gun to his (her) shoulder at the sporting goods counter, chances are it'll do the job. At the same time, any prospective scattergun buyer should handle and heft several different models before making a final choice. If one feels noticeably better, that's the one he should probably buy. Even the standard stocks vary slightly in thickness and size, and

Shotguns are designed to hit moving targets at close range.

some guns will simply handle better than others.

Shotgun Types

There are six different types of shotguns available: slide action (pump), autoloader, side-by-side double barrel, over-under double barrel, bolt action, and break-top single shot. To make the choice even more difficult, there are a half-dozen different gauges to choose from: 10, 12, 16, 20, 28 and .410. What's more, shotguns are offered in several different barrel lengths, and those barrels can be choked in a number of different ways. Choke refers to the constriction at the shotgun's muzzle that controls the way the shot pattern spreads. Like the nozzle on a garden hose, a shotgun's choke can be designed to emit a wide, fine spray, or shoot a tightly clustered column of shot that doesn't begin to appreciably spread out for 25 or 30 yards.

With all these variables to consider, choosing a hunting shotgun doesn't appear to be a simple chore. In practice, the selection usually isn't very difficult. Shotguns are purchased more on the basis of personal preference than on any other criteria. People who like the way double-barreled shotguns look and feel *buy* double guns. Other shooters buy pumpguns or autoloaders for the very same reasons. The choice often depends on what the gunner is already used to.

The fact is, the action type of the gun you buy has little to do with your success in the field. An over-under double gun can be as deadly in the duck blind as a long-barreled autoloader, and a pump or side-by-side will do just as well. There are few hard-and-fast rules to go by.

Each shotgun type has its own advantages and disadvantages, and these are worth listing here. The autoloader offers fast repeat shots, and all the gunner has to do is pull and release the trigger each time he wants to shoot. The primary advantage autoloaders have over other shotgun types is their ability to reduce felt recoil. The autoloader's gas-operated action spreads recoil forces out over a longer time span, and this eases the jolt to the shooter's shoulder. Because of this, the autoloader makes a good choice where heavy, magnum loads are used. Ithaca's 10-gauge Mag-10 autoloader is the only 10-gauge on the market that could be described as pleasant to shoot, and many waterfowlers who need the reach a 12-gauge magnum provides prefer autoloaders for their relative comfort.

On the negative side, autoloaders can be fussy when it comes to digesting reloaded or handloaded ammunition. Too, such guns are longer and more muzzle-heavy than are short-coupled doubles. The reciprocating action

There are six different types of shotguns available: **1.** pump (Remington 870 shown), **2.** Autoloader (Browning B-80), **3.** Side-by-side double (Stevens 311), **4.** Over-under (Ruger over-under), **5.** Bolt action (Marlin Model 444), and **6.** Break-top single shot (Harrington & Richardson Topper)

adds several inches to the gun's overall length. If the gun is fitted with a 28-, 30-, or 32-inch barrel, it becomes a very long firearm. Long, muzzle-heavy guns can help slow and stabilize the swing needed to lead and kill high-flying waterfowl, but they're not as fast and responsive as other guns in hunting upland game. Because autoloaders *do* automatically reload themselves as soon as each shot is fired, they're not the best choice for young hunters or beginners. It's too easy for an inexperienced shooter to forget that another round is chambered and ready to shoot. All it takes is another pull on the trigger.

The pump, or slide-action repeater, is likely the most popular shotgun type among American hunters. Like the autoloader, the pumpgun offers several rapid repeat shots in reserve—but the chamber isn't reloaded until you manually shuck that sliding fore-end. Many shooters prefer a manually operated action, and an ex-

perienced trombone gun operator can trigger off follow-up shots as fast as most autoloader owners can.

As far as length and balance are concerned, the same remarks used for auto shotguns apply. Either can be fast handling with short 20- or 24-inch barrels but become progressively less lively as barrel length increases.

The slide action makes a good, solid, reliable repeater, and most models are very reasonably priced. This doesn't hurt its popularity.

Traditionalists prefer the side-by-side double, which, as its name implies, features twin barrels in horizontal alignment. Because double-barreled guns lack a reciprocating action, they're shorter overall than a magazine-fed repeater of the same barrel length. This makes doubles fast and lively, and a lightweight side-by-side makes it possible to "get on" close-flushing birds much quicker.

Another advantage is the fact that a twin-

The choke constriction in a shotgun's muzzle determines how quickly the pattern spreads.

The primary advantage autoloaders have over other shotgun types is their ability to reduce felt recoil.

The pump, or slide-action, is the most popular shotgun type. Here author Rees shoots Ithaca M-37 Featherlight.

Side-by-side doubles are the choice of many "traditionalists." Such guns offer fine balance and the instant choice of two degrees of choke. Gun is Browning BSS.

tubed shotgun gives you the instant choice between two different degrees of choke. If one barrel is choked "modified" and the other bored "full," you can fire the full-choked tube first if a bird flushes wild at 40 yards. Conversely, the wider shot pattern thrown by the modified-choked barrel is ideal for closer targets. Some budget-priced models don't allow you to choose the firing sequence; these single-trigger guns always fire the more open-choked barrel first, which works fine if the target is flying away from you. Other doubles have single selective triggers, which can be quickly reset to reverse the sequence, while

some double-barreled guns sport not one, but two triggers, each controlling a separate barrel.

Disadvantages include the fact that side-by-side doubles sport such a broad sighting plane that it's possible to "cross shoot," or view the target at an angle along the twin barrels. This can cause a miss because of improper alignment. If the stock is properly positioned, this won't happen. Many inexpensive doubles have simple extractors that merely lift the fired (and unfired) shells a short distance from their chambers, where they must be removed by hand. This slows the reloading process but allows handloaders to retrieve empties without chasing them all over the countryside. More costly models feature selective automatic ejectors that kick empty hulls clear of the gun while leaving unfired shells in their chambers when the action is opened.

Over-under shotguns, with their twin barrels stacked one atop the other, have much in common with the more traditional side-by-side doubles. The same comments apply, except for the fact that the slimmer, single-barrel sighting plane that the stackbarrel presents is favored by most modern shooters. Too, the recoil of the lower barrel lies directly in line with the buttstock, which is pushed straight back into the shooter's shoulder. On a side-by-side double, both barrels lie slightly off center, and recoil forces the gun minutely right or left. This can slam the buttstock a fraction of an inch sideways, into or away from the shooter's cheek—and this can cause bruising with heavy loads. If the gun fits the shooter, neither type of double-barreled firearm is unpleasant to shoot. But all other things being equal, the over-under is less likely to punish the gunner.

Bolt-action shotguns are the least expensive repeating shotguns on the market. They're reliable, but ungainly and unlovely to look at. They lack the fine, fast-handling balance of many scatterguns, but they'll get the job done if aesthetics aren't important to you.

While single-shot trap guns can be of very high quality and are favored by many target competitors, most one-shooters used for hunting are budget-priced models. Their main sell-

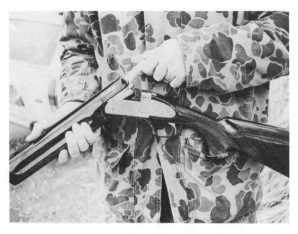

Over-under or stackbarrel shotguns offer two fast shots and a single sighting plane.

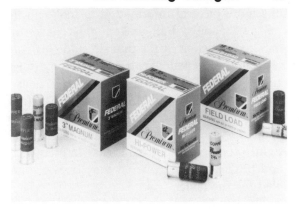

The 12-gauge is the overwhelming favorite of hunters. Twelve-gauge guns with 3-inch chambers can shoot 3-inch heavy magnum loads, at left, 1¼-ounce express loads, or light 1⅛-ounce field loads.

ing point is low cost. The fact that they shoot but a single shot at a time before reloading is necessary makes these guns good choices for youths or beginners.

Shotgun Gauges

While there are a half-dozen different shotgun gauges available, modern bird hunters almost invariably choose 12- or 20-gauge guns. Shotgun bore size was originally measured by the number of lead balls, sized to just fit the bore, that it took to scale a pound. If 10 lead balls the size of the bore weighed a pound, the gun was a 10-gauge. Thus the larger the "gauge" number, the smaller the bore size.

Today, 10-gauge shotguns are used almost exclusively for pass shooting at high-flying geese and ducks, or for turkey hunting. These guns are too large and heavy for the upland game field and, except for the Ithaca Mag-10 autoloader already mentioned, kick entirely too hard for comfort.

The 12-gauge is the overwhelming favorite of hunters everywhere. With standard loads, it's capable of throwing 1¼ ounces of shot, and 3-inch magnum 12s hold as much as 1⅞ ounces. The more shot a scattergun can put in the air, the greater the pattern density and the longer the effective range.

At one time, the 16-gauge was highly popular among American bird hunters, with the 20 following in its wake. With the advent of the 3-inch magnum 20-gauge shotshell, the Sweet Sixteen fell from favor and has been almost entirely replaced by the 20. Sixteen-gauge guns are still a fine choice for nearly all bird hunting, but this gauge is becoming so rare that ammunition may be hard to find in some out-of-the-way spots.

The 3-inch magnum 20 holds 1¼ ounces of shot, while the standard 2¾-inch load contains an even ounce. The 1-ounce load is perfectly adequate for hunting upland game, and the magnum 20 is the ballistic equal of the non-magnum 12 for hunting waterfowl or late-season ringnecks. Twenty-gauge guns are typically lighter than their 12-gauge sisters, which means they're faster handling.

The 28-gauge is currently loaded with but ¾ ounce of shot, and the even smaller .410 throws 11/16 ounces when you use 3-inch shells. The standard 2½-inch .410 fodder contains only a half ounce of pellets. Both of these smallbores will kill birds if the range is right, but they're not ideal for the hunting field.

Gun Chokes

Choke has already been mentioned, but with the several degrees of choke available you need one more piece of information to make an intelligent choice. Full-choked guns have the most constriction at the muzzle, and this concentrates the pellet pattern for long-range shooting. Full-choked guns throw a dense-enough pattern to kill birds at 45 or 50 yards, but that same pattern is really *too* dense for good 30-yard shooting. At short range, the tightly constricted pattern is easy to miss with, and birds that *are* centered may be too mangled for the table.

The modified choke is for medium range: from 25 to 40 yards or so. The improved cylinder throws a still wider pattern for 20-to-35-yard shooting. At longer ranges, the pellet concentration will be too thin for consistent kills. A straight cylinder-choked gun has no constriction at all at the muzzle: it's good out to 30 yards and is deadly at close range. Shotgun barrels designed to shoot rifled slugs in the deer woods usually wear cylinder chokes, and these "deer gun" tubes work well for hunting quail and other tight-holding upland game when used with shotshells.

Barrel length has little effect on shot velocity, and shotgun barrels are available in 20-, 22-, 24-, 26-, 28-, 30-, 32-, and 36-inch lengths. The short barrels make for very quick handling, while the longer tubes help smooth the swing. Longer barrels are also a bit quieter, as the muzzle blast takes place farther from the ear. The most common barrel lengths are from 26 to 30 inches, with the longer barrels usually wearing tighter chokes. Most pumps and autoloaders allow you to buy extra barrels and interchange them so you can make use of whatever choke you feel the hunting situation demands. Or you can have a Poly-Choke or some other adjustable choke device fitted to the muzzle of your gun; this lets you vary the choke constriction by simply twisting a collet. An increasing number of production shotguns are now being factory-fitted with interchange-

For hunting deer, rifled slug loads are available. These shoot a single, heavy lead slug in place of the usual multiple-pellet shot charge.

able-choke-tube muzzle devices, and these add much to a shotgun's utility.

Choosing Shot Size

Once you've selected your shotgun type, gauge, choke constriction, and barrel length, you still have to decide what kind of ammunition to feed your gun. Shotgun shells are available loaded with solid, "rifled" slugs and buckshot, but these combinations are for deer or other large or medium-sized game. The smallest buckshot (No. 4 Buck) may be used for high-flying geese, but that's its only practical bird-shooting utility.

Bird hunters can choose from shot sizes ranging from BB (the largest size) to 8½ and 9 (the smallest). Since shotshells are loaded by weight, the smaller the shot size used, the greater the number of pellets in each load. Using small shot gives dense patterns, but larger, heavier pellets fly farther and give better penetration. As a rule, small shot is used for small birds, while large tough-skinned birds like geese require larger pellets. Use the accompanying shotshell selector chart to determine the best shot sizes for the game being hunted.

Shotshell Guide

SHOT PATTERNS AND CHOKE

The amount of constriction in a gun's muzzle is referred to as the "choke." Different amounts of constriction give different-sized patterns to a shot charge. For example, a "full choke" forces the shot charge closer together as it leaves the gun, delaying the tendency of the shot to spread. As a result, a "full choke" pattern is effective at greater distances. At close range, however, a "full choke" pattern may be too small to ensure being on target, or so dense that the game is ruined.

FULL CHOKE:

Shot pattern effective at long range up to 50 to 55 yards, but too small and too dense at short range.

MODIFIED CHOKE:

Best pattern at medium range. 25 to 45 yards.

IMPROVED CYLINDER:

Excellent for short range up to 30 to 35 yards, but pattern may be too thin at long range to ensure enough hits.

NO.	9	8½	8	7½	6	5	4	2	1	BB
SHOT SIZES	•	•	●	●	●	●	●	●	●	●
Diameter in inches	.08	.085	.09	.095	.11	.12	.13	.15	.16	.18

BUCKSHOT	No.4	No.3	No.2	No.1	No.0	No.00	No.000
Diameter in inches	.24	.25	.27	.30	.32	.33	.36

SHOT PELLETS PER OUNCE (Approximate)

LEAD				STEEL	
Size	Pellets	Size	Pellets	Size	Pellets
BB	50	6	225	BB	72
2	87	7½	350	1	103
4	135	8	410	2	125
5	170	9	585	4	192

Courtesy Federal Cartridge Corp.

RANGE

Waterfowl hunting usually involves the longest distances for shotgun shooting. The practical range for taking ducks and geese is 35 to 50 yards.

Individual pellets, however, may travel great distances. For safety when hunting, consider these possible extreme ranges.

00 Buck	610 yds.
No. 2 Shot	337 yds.
No. 6 Shot	275 yds.
No. 9 Shot	225 yds.

THE SHOTSHELL SELECTOR
Lead Shot Unless Indicated "Steel"

	Type of Shell	Size
DUCKS	Magnum or Hi-Power	4,5,6 Steel 2,4
GEESE	Magnum or Hi-Power	BB,2,4 Steel BB,1,2,
PHEASANTS	Magnum or Hi-Power	5,6,7½
QUAIL	Hi-Power or Field Load	7½,8,9
RUFFED GROUSE & HUNGARIAN PARTRIDGE	Hi-Power or Field Load	6,7½,8
OTHER GROUSE CHUKAR PARTRIDGE	Hi-Power or Field Load	5,6,7½
DOVES & PIGEONS	Hi-Power or Field Load	6,7½,8,9
RABBITS	Hi-Power or Field Load	4,5,6,7½
WOODCOCK, SNIPE, RAIL	Field Load	7½,8,9
SQUIRRELS	Hi-Power or Field Load	4,5,6
WILD TURKEYS	Magnum or Hi-Power	2,4,5,6
CROWS	Hi-Power or Field Load	5,6,7½
FOXES	Magnum or Hi-Power	BB,2,4

DRAMS EQUIVALENT NUMBER
Example 3-1/4 Drams Equivalent

This guide number, found on shotshell boxes, gives the weight of black powder used in the past to obtain established velocities for each load. Black powder is no longer used, so the figure does not represent the actual amount of modern smokeless powder now used.

6

The Hunting Handgun

Handguns are increasingly being used by hunters who want to add extra challenge to their sport. Hunters of rabbits, squirrels, and other small game have long used rimfire revolvers and auto pistols from time to time when the range wasn't too demanding. Varmint hunters who imitate a rabbit's distress cry to lure predators to them have used handguns with great success.

There have also been a limited number of skilled nimrods who have regularly killed deer with magnum six-guns. In recent years that number has increased dramatically, and most states now recognize certain magnum handguns as legal deer-hunting equipment.

The heightened interest in handgun hunting has led to the development of new, highly specialized guns. Break-top single-shot pistols chambered for any number of high-velocity, flat-shooting cartridges are now selling well.

With a long-eye-relief scope sight mounted and in skilled hands, such handguns are capable of surprising accuracy out to 200 yards or more. Chambered for rifle-type rounds of high potency, some of these one-shooters are capable of tackling game much larger than deer. As a matter of fact, just about every type of game that walks the earth has now been hunted with a handgun—with varying success.

Almost any handgun can be used for hunting, but there are certain limitations that must be observed. Rimfire handguns shooting .22 short, long, or long rifle ammunition, or guns chambered for the more potent .22 magnum rimfire are suitable for only the smallest of game. This includes rabbits and squirrels, and other critters of similar size. Possums and raccoons are favorite targets of rimfire-toting handgunners; these animals are often shot from their trees at relatively close range. Rac-

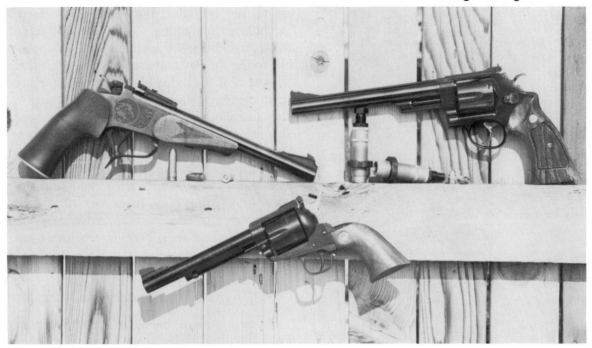

Clockwise from left, Thompson/Center Contender break-top single shot, Smith & Wesson double-action revolver, and Ruger Blackhawk single-action revolver—all are chambered for magnum rounds potent enough for hunting deer and other large game.

coon hunters often walk many miles between shots, and favor light handguns that can be carried holstered on the hip, where they're out of the way until needed. A holstered handgun lets the hunter keep both hands free—a big point in favor of carrying a pistol or revolver instead of a bulky rifle.

Because handguns *can* be kept out of the way until it's time to use them, they're favored by houndmen who run behind their dogs until their quarry trees. For some kinds of hunting, handguns are simply more practical than rifles or shotguns.

Most sportsmen who turn to the handgun for hunting are simply trying to make things tougher for themselves. The handgun is basically a short-range tool, and the average six-gunner tries to stalk within 50 or 75 yards of a deer before attempting to shoot. Many get much closer. By law, most deer hunters are limited to single-shot pistols or revolvers firing a .357, .41, or .44 magnum cartridge. Some single-shot pistols are chambered for even more potent rifle cartridges, and these are legal too. Even the big .44 magnum handgun round lacks the punch to kill deer-sized animals cleanly much farther than 70 or 80 yards from the muzzle. Halving that distance before you shoot is wise insurance.

For small-game handgunning, Ruger's .22 rimfire auto pistol is a fine choice.

High Standard .22 auto pistol is a great gun for hunting western jackrabbits.

Handguns used for hunting should have barrels no shorter than 4 inches in length, and 6- or 8-inch barrels are even better. Longer barrels provide increased velocity and a longer sighting plane. They also weigh more, and this makes the guns more controllable and easier to shoot. This is particularly important when shooting a big-bore magnum.

Handgun Sights

A good set of adjustable, target-type sights are required for a hunting handgun. It's important to be able to adjust those sights to accommodate the particular brand of ammunition and bullet weight used. Changing bullet weights or varying the load can drastically change the point of impact at 40 or 50 yards. The sights should be easy to see, even under poor lighting conditions.

Many hunters now add magnifying scopes to their handguns. This addition increases the gun's bulk and weight but provides a clearer picture of the target. With conventional open sights, the eye tries to rapidly switch focus through three sighting planes: the rear sight, the front sight, and the target. This is impossible, so the shooter must settle on having either the target or the sights blur in his vision. Since sight alignment is so very important with a short-barreled handgun, most experienced shooters opt to let the target blur and concentrate on seeing the sights clearly. With an optical scope sight, this isn't necessary. You simply look through the scope reticle, and superimpose the sighting cross hairs over the target. The junction of those narrow cross hairs also provides greater spot-shooting precision than the relatively coarse open sights allow.

Handgun Accessories

Hunting with a handgun requires greater marksmanship skills than a rifleman must have. This means long hours of pre-season

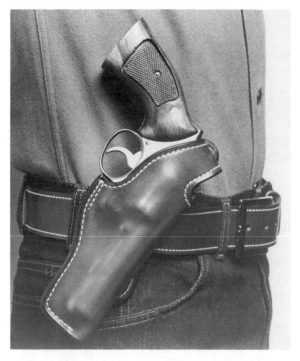

Because handguns can be kept holstered and out of the way until needed, they're favored by those who hunt with hounds and would prefer not to be burdened by a rifle.

Long-barreled handguns provide increased velocity and a longer sighting plane for better accuracy with open sights.

Many handgunners now add magnifying scope sights to their guns. Rees's .44 magnum Ruger Redhawk revolver sports a 2X Leupold pistol scope.

practice and a genuine desire to learn to shoot well. A set of close-fitting muff-type ear protectors or shooter's earplugs are required during practice; without such protection, your hearing will soon suffer permanent loss. Also, it's almost impossible to shoot a magnum handgun during a long practice session without developing a nasty, accuracy-destroying flinch. Hardened eyeglasses or safety lenses are also recommended; these will protect your eyes from spitting lead and escaping gases.

Hunters invariably shoot their handguns using a firm, two-handed grip. Whenever possible, they take advantage of trees, stumps, boulders, and other natural rests to help steady their aim. The gun is never rested directly against such hard, unyielding objects, as this could jar the gun and send the bullet off course. Instead, the shooter's hands are steadied against the object.

Handgun Shooting Positions

Like riflemen, handgunners also drop into a sitting, kneeling, or prone shooting position whenever there's the time and the opportunity.

Smith & Wesson model 57 with 8³/₈-inch barrel and target-style sights is a fine deer-hunting revolver in .41 Remington Magnum chambering.

Hunters invariably shoot their handguns using a firm, two-handed grip. Belt holster is made by Don Hume.

Shooting while standing offers little stability, and the handgunner needs all the steadiness he or she can get. The sitting position is the favorite of most handgunning hunters. It's steady, comfortable, and easy to assume. It also keeps the gun and sights high enough to let the shooter see over low brush and undergrowth. To get into the sitting position, simply sit down facing the target, with your legs spread a comfortable distance apart and the knees bent. Pull your knees up until you can lean forward and rest the lower portion of your upper arms (the area just behind the elbows) just forward of your upraised knees. (Placing the elbows directly on the kneecaps is uncomfortable and unsteady.) Hold the gun in a two-handed grip directly in front of you, pointing at the target.

Types of Handguns

Both single-action and double-action handguns are suitable for hunting. Single-action guns must be manually cocked before they'll fire, while double-action guns can be fired by simply pulling their triggers. Double-action re-

For deer-sized game, the .357 magnum (CENTER) is the legal minimum handgun load in most states. Heavier .41 and .44 magnums are more potent, and better killers.

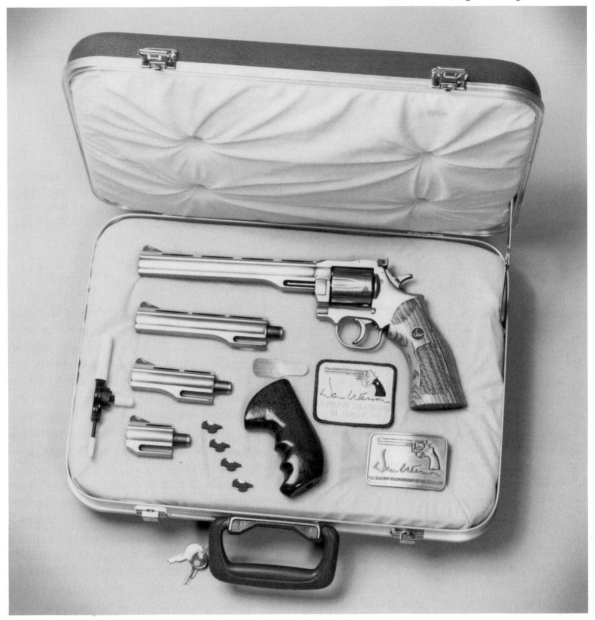

Dan Wesson revolvers feature readily interchangeable barrels of different lengths and are available in both small-game and deer-hunting calibers.

volvers can also be manually cocked and fired single action, if desired. Since single-action shooting provides a more easily controlled trigger pull and better accuracy, hunters almost invariably use this mode.

Any number of rimfire auto pistols, revolvers, and single shots are suitable for small-game hunting. Charter Arms' Pathfinder re-

volver is available with either a 3-inch or a 6-inch barrel, and the 3-inch version may be the smallest practical rimfire revolver for serious sporting use. Colt, Smith & Wesson, Harrington & Richardson, Dan Wesson, Interarms, Ruger, and others all offer several .22 revolvers with barrels ranging from 4 to 8 and even 10 inches. Ruger, Colt, Iver Johnson,

Specialized bolt-action single-shot handguns like this Wichita Classic model chamber flat-shooting rifle cartridges and are suitable for big game out to 200 yards or more in the hands of a skilled marksman.

Shot-loaded cartridges are available that turn big-bore handguns into mini-shotguns for close-range bird shooting. James Rees shot this forest grouse with a shot-loaded .44 magnum revolver.

Browning, and Smith & Wesson rimfire auto pistols are also excellent choices. Rimfire single shots are available from Thompson/Center Corporation.

Handgun Cartridges

Revolvers and auto pistols chambered for such medium-powered cartridges as the .32 and .38 Special, the .380 ACP, the 9mm Parabellum, and the .38 Super are all fine for small animals like foxes and rabbits but lack the necessary oomph for larger game like deer and antelope.

For deer-sized game, the .357 magnum is the legal minimum in many states. Most sportsmen prefer even more potency and opt for something like the longer .357 Maximum or big-bores like the .41 and .44 Remington magnums. These are all fine short-range hunting rounds.

The Thompson/Center Contender and other single shots like those offered by Wichita Arms are available in a variety of chamberings, including the magnum loads just mentioned. These guns feature barrels 10 inches or longer in length and milk the maximum velocities from these loads. Some of these one-shooters are also chambered for even more potent rifle cartridges and shoot flat enough to take game out to 200 yards or so.

Shot-loaded cartridges are also available in some handgun calibers. These loads contain multiple tiny shot pellets in a frangible plastic projectile that breaks apart in flight to release the pellets. This gives a shotgun effect, and it's possible to kill birds with these loads at short range. Few sportsmen hunt birds seriously with a handgun. Most birds taken by handgun shot loads are killed for the pot by deer-hunting handgunners who had the foresight to bring a few of these specialized cartridges along.

Like bow hunters, nimrods who use a handgun to take their game are doing things the hard way. Hunting with either of these short-range weapons adds greatly to the challenge of the sport—but also increases the satisfaction of success.

7

Bow Hunting

Bow hunting began many centuries ago and remains today a highly popular sport. To the modern archer, taking game offers a real challenge. To succeed, he must know the habits of the game he is hunting and how to take advantage of the terrain. He must be a skilled stalker and an even more skillful archer.

Bow hunting is the most primitive of the hunting sports—and one of the most truly satisfying. By depending on an ancient weapon, the twentieth-century archer steps back in time and gains a fresh appreciation of his hunting heritage. Because bow hunters are far fewer in number than their rifle-toting brethren, they enjoy much greater solitude. During regular deer season, popular hunting areas may be crowded with orange-clad riflemen. This detracts from the hunting experience, and in some cases can even cause safety concerns. Archers have their own special season, and hunt virtually alone.

If the bowman fails to down his buck during archery season, he has a second chance when the regular hunting season rolls around.

Bow hunting isn't limited to the deer woods. Elk, moose, and other large game regularly fall to well-placed arrows, and considerably smaller marks like rabbits and squirrels are also fair game to the archer. Even flying game like pheasants and grouse are taken every year by bow-packing sportsmen.

Bow hunting is truly a year-round sport. In the spring and summer months, many archers attach reels to their equipment and go bow fishing. Carp and other rough fish make large, sporting targets in shallow water, while coastal archers hunt sharks, rays, and other species.

The basic equipment that a bow hunter needs includes a bow, a supply of broadhead-equipped arrows, some kind of quiver, an armguard, and an archery glove. Most experienced bowmen also consider camouflage cloth-

Bow hunting is a year-round sport. In spring and summer months, many archers attach reels to their bows and go bow fishing for carp and other rough fish. (BEAR ARCHERY PHOTO)

Bow hunting isn't limited to the deer woods. Caribou and other large and/or exotic game have fallen to archers all over the world. (BEAR ARCHERY PHOTO)

ing and face paint necessary to help them stalk close enough to get the job done.

Bow Types

There are several different kinds of hunting bows available, in a variety of price ranges and quality. The lemonwood or yew English longbow that dominated archery for several centuries still exists but has virtually disappeared from the hunting scene. It was largely replaced in the 1930s by the modern recurve bow, a design inspired by the short, tip-curved Turkish bows used in the days of the Roman Empire. The recurve bow provided greater energy than the longbow did, and provided a smoother, easier draw. Today's recurve bows

are made of fiberglass-laminated hardwood. These are excellent for hunting, and they cost less than the newer compound designs.

Compound bows began appearing in the 1970s. Millions are now in use. The compound bow uses a system of pulleys to store draw power, and it reduces the energy needed to bring the bow to full draw. This design also throws arrows 10 to 15 percent faster than a recurve bow of similar draw weight.

The latest compound designs utilize eccentric wheels to provide even easier draws and greater power. These ultramodern bows are very complicated in appearance, with cables crisscrossing several times between the limbs. But they work very well. Compound bows are made of both laminated hardwood and fiberglass and may have handles made of magnesium or other lightweight alloys. These bows are excellent but relatively expensive.

Bows are available in many different draw weights, but hunters should select a model drawing at least 45 pounds. That means it requires 45 pounds of pressure to pull the arrow to full draw. That weight is the minimum required for hunting deer in many states, and many hunters choose a 50-, 55-, or 60-pound

Most experienced bowmen—and women—consider camouflage clothing a necessity to help them stalk within archery range of animals.

model. Heavier bow weights are available, but it takes a great deal of practice and a certain amount of sheer strength to master even a 60-pound pull. Beginning archers are better off with a 45-, 50-, or 55-pound hunting bow.

Today's hunting arrows are made of cedar, fiberglass, or aluminum. Cedar arrows are the least expensive and will do a good job in the deer woods when fitted with sharp broadheads. Arrows with fiberglass shafts cost more but are more durable and weatherproof. They're also heavier than cedar shafts, adding weight for

better penetration. Aluminum arrows are becoming increasingly popular among bow hunters; these are very durable and are available in a variety of grades. Graphite and other materials are also used.

Arrows should be "spined," or matched to the proper stiffness for your bow. If you're using a bow with a 50-pound draw weight, the arrows should be spined to match that pull. Arrows are also available in various lengths and should be about an inch longer than your draw length. To determine your draw length,

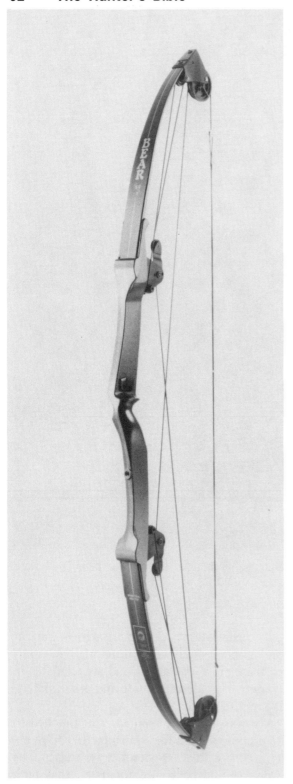

The recurve bow provides greater energy than the outmoded longbow and is an excellent choice for hunting. (BEAR ARCHERY PHOTO)

hold a yardstick projecting from the center of your chest and clasp your hands against it with your arms and fingers fully extended. The draw length can be measured at your fingertips. Another method is to stand facing a wall with the knuckles of your clenched fist against the wall and your arm fully extended. The draw length is measured from the corner of your mouth to the place where your knuckles meet the wall.

Broadheads and Quivers

A variety of different hunting broadheads are available, and most are highly effective on game. The chief requirement is that they be razor sharp. A dull broadhead simply won't penetrate into an animal and get the job done. Blunt field points are also needed for practice, and these should match your broadheads in weight. Arrowheads are attached to the arrow

Compound bows use a system of pulleys to store draw power, reducing the energy needed to bring a bow to and hold it at full draw.

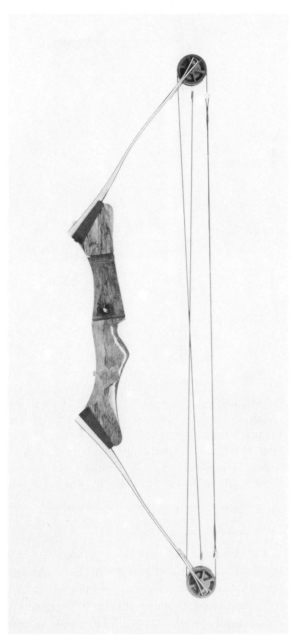

Bow quivers keep arrowheads sharp and place several arrows close at hand for fast shooting.

Browning's X-cellerator compound bow throws arrows 20 to 15 percent faster than a recurve bow of similar draw weight.

shafts by ferrule cement or screwed into a fitting that has been cemented in place. Arrows with easily interchangeable points are much more versatile than the cement-on variety, as the same shaft can be used for target practice or hunting.

Quivers are also available in a variety of designs. These strap to the archer's back, fasten to his belt, or attach directly to the bow itself. The vast majority of hunters use bow quivers, as these offer good arrow protection, are out of the way, and make fast follow-up shots possible.

Other Bow Accessories

Bow sights are also popular accessories. These consist of a set of aiming pins used as reference points and can be adjusted for various shooting ranges. Many bow hunters, though, still prefer to shoot "instinctively," without the use of sights. Good results are possible with either method.

Armguards and archery gloves are used to protect the inside of the sportsman's forearm

TYPES OF ARROWS

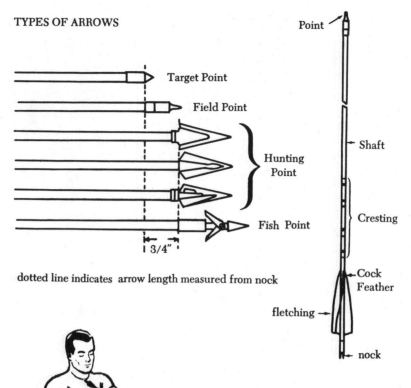

Target Point

Field Point

Hunting Point

Fish Point

3/4"

dotted line indicates arrow length measured from nock

Point

Shaft

Cresting

Cock Feather

fletching →

nock

Good-quality arrows shoot straighter and last longer. When buying an arrow, you can gauge your requirements by seeing if the arrow will reach from your chest to your fingertips when held as illustrated. The standard is 28″ because the average adult armspan is best suited to this draw size.

from the string as it snaps forward, and to guard the three shooting fingers from abrasion as the bowstring is released.

Other useful accessories include string silencers or dampeners to eliminate noisy "twang" when the bowstring is released, dull paint to camouflage the bow, screw-in stabilizers to improve accuracy, and, of course, bowstring wax for prolonged string life.

Shooting for Results

The best way to learn good bow-shooting technique is to enlist the aid of an experienced archer. Learn the proper stance and the other fundamentals, then practice regularly on both bull's-eye targets and animal silhouettes.

Right-handed archers should grasp the bow in their left hand and stand with their left side toward the target. The feet should be a comfortable distance apart, the body at nearly a right angle to the target. The bow handle should be grasped lightly but firmly, and the shooter's body should be erect and relaxed.

The arrow should be laid across the arrow rest located in the sighting notch just above the bow handle. The nock should be fitted to the bowstring immediately above the nock set or locator button. If two locating buttons are used, the nock should rest between them. The odd-colored feather or plastic vane is called the cock feather; this should be pointing away from the bow handle, or to the left for a right-handed archer.

Master archer Fred Bear with compound hunting bow fitted with bow quiver. He's wearing an archery glove and arm guard to prevent abrasion from the bowstring. (BEAR ARCHERY PHOTO)

Bow sights are popular accessories. These consist of aiming pins that can be adjusted for various shooting ranges.

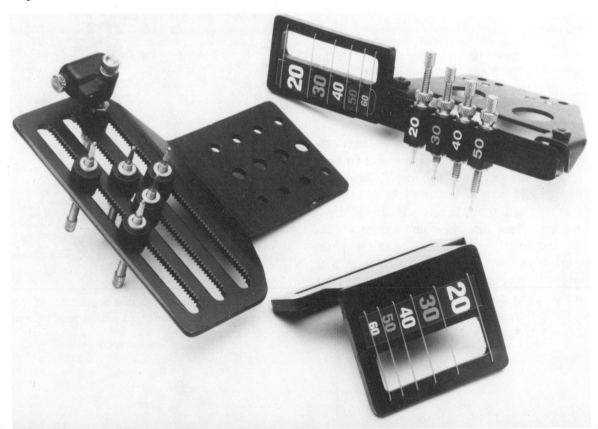

With the bow extended full length toward the target, the bowstring is drawn back alongside the face and "anchored" there. The bowstring should be anchored in exactly the same spot each time.

The string is grasped with the index finger above the arrow nock, and the two middle fingers below it. These three fingers should be protected by a shooting glove or tab. The string is held by either the first joints or pads of the fingers.

With the bow arm extended full length toward the target, the bowstring is drawn back alongside the face and "anchored" there. The bowstring should be anchored in exactly the same spot each time the arrow is drawn; this is very important for consistent accuracy. The bow should be vertical, and the elbow of the right, or bowstring arm should be level with the shoulders during the draw so that the back and shoulder muscles—not the arm muscles—do the pulling.

If a bowsight is used, the archer uses one of the sight pins as an aiming reference. The pin or pins should be adjusted to produce hits when the pin covers the target at certain known yardages. The instinctive shooter uses no accessory sight or artificial reference point. He simply releases the arrow when the bow angle looks or feels right. Either method can produce results.

The bow is held at full draw while aiming takes place, which is one reason a too-heavy bow is undesirable. If an archer must strain to hold the arrow at full draw, the shot will be hurried and liable to miss. The bowstring must be held firmly at its anchor point, and neither pulled farther back nor allowed to slip forward just before it's released. The proper way to release the arrow is to simply relax the three fingers holding the bowstring and allow the string to slip smoothly forward.

Follow through is also very important. The bow should be held as still as possible and in the same position until the arrow is well on its way. Any movement of the bow before the arrow clears it will cause a miss.

The key to bow-hunting success is practice—lots of it. Use arrows and points that match your hunting arrows in weight.

A deer hit by an arrow may travel a hundred yards or more before succumbing. A short search along the animal's trail should bring success. (BEAR ARCHERY PHOTO)

Once the standard shooting stance is mastered, you should try shooting from various other field positions—kneeling, shooting downhill from a tree stand, at uphill targets, and through or around screening brush. Try your hand at moving targets, too—a piece of cardboard attached to a rolling tire helps you judge the lead necessary to hit running game.

Don't make the mistake of shooting at the entire animal when you finally go afield. Aim for a single, vital point. Just behind the front shoulder midway down the body is the best place to aim at a deer standing broadside. Try to puncture the heart and/or lungs. Once you've hit a deer or other large animal with an arrow, don't immediately chase after it. Arrows kill by hemorrhaging, not by shock. Give the animal a few minutes to lie down and stiffen up before you follow its trail. Once you've put an arrow into an animal, stay on its trail until you've found it. A vitally wounded deer may travel several hundred yards before it succumbs.

The key to bow-hunting success is practice

—lots of it. Bales of hay make an excellent target backstop when you're shooting field-pointed arrows. If the arrow hasn't penetrated up to the fletching, it can be withdrawn by flattening your hand against the target with your splayed fingers on either side of the arrow and using your other hand to pull the arrow free. If you insist on shooting broadheads into baled hay, the arrows must be pushed on through and out the other side; it's almost impossible to withdraw them without losing the broadhead in the hay.

Learn the ranges at which you can consistently place arrows in the bull's-eye, then limit your shooting to game at these ranges. Fifty yards is a long shot for most archers. Your best bet is to get in close and make that first arrow count. Chances are you'll not have time for a second shot.

8

Hunting with Muzzle-loaders

Like bow hunters, sportsmen who use muzzle-loading firearms to take game are heavily dependent on stalking skills. Black-powder hunting rifles will kill game farther than a bow and arrow will but have nowhere near the range of a modern, high-velocity smokeless powder sporter.

Because they typically carry wide-open, straight-cylinder chokes, black-powder shotguns suffer similar range limitations when compared to modern bird guns. Too, the hand-crafted-on-the-spot black-powder loads aren't nearly as efficient as today's shotshells.

In addition to those drawbacks, muzzle-loading rifles and shotguns are ponderously slow to reload. If you're using a black-powder rifle, that first shot must count. If it only wounds, you must load the rifle again and track the animal down to get another shot. A modern repeater places fast second, third, or even fourth follow-up shots at your disposal.

Double-barreled black-powder bird guns let you shoot twice before reloading, but if you miss or a third bird gets up you're out of luck. If it's raining or snowing, reloading can be a slow, messy, miserable process. If the powder becomes damp, it won't fire and must be augered out of the bore and replaced with a fresh load.

With all these disadvantages to contend with, why do so many people hunt with muzzle-loading firearms? Like bow hunters, they like the added challenge. Nostalgia plays a big part, too, and many black-powder buffs dress in buckskins and other backwoods costumes dating back a century or more.

Hunters who use muzzle-loading firearms afield do so simply to add more fun to their

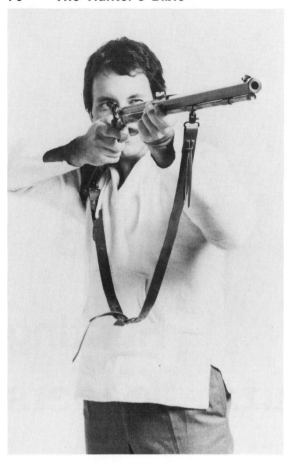

Modern muzzle-loaders are popular among many American hunters.

enjoy. Of course, these same primitive firearms may also be used during the regular season.

While a few sportsmen own and use antique firearms made a century ago, most hunters purchase one of the modern replicas available from Thompson/Center, Navy Arms, Browning, Connecticut Valley Arms, and others. Both flintlock and percussion lock rifles are used to hunt with, but the percussion lock firearms are more convenient and more reliable, and therefore more popular.

Loading Muzzle-loaders

Except for the priming, both flintlock and percussion rifles are loaded pretty much the same. First, the priming pan or percussion nipple is checked to make sure no powder or percussion cap is in place. This helps guard against accidental discharge during the loading procedure—an event that could have tragic effect on the loader.

Next, a measured charge of black powder or its modern substitute, Pyrodex, is poured

sport. They gain satisfaction from loading their guns in the old-fashioned, step-by-step way, and enjoy the acrid cloud of black-powder smoke that invariably masks the target whenever the guns are fired.

Though black-powder hunting guns aren't as efficient as their modern counterparts, they remain surprisingly effective. A .50- or .54-caliber rifle slug or ball is a deadly killer on deer- or elk-sized game, while muzzle-loading scatterguns work just fine at typical upland gamebird ranges. Guns like these put meat on the table for centuries, and they'll still do the trick. All they ask is to be used at sensible ranges.

Some states offer special hunting seasons for black-powder riflemen, giving muzzle-loading buffs much the same status that bow hunters

Modern percussion rifles are capable of excellent accuracy.

Shooting black-powder rifles requires certain accessories: special cleaner and solvent, a supply of Pyrodex or black powder, lead balls of the proper caliber, ramrod (on gun), patches, capper, and nipple wrench.

down the bore. FFG granulated black powder is commonly used for rifles of from .45 to .58 caliber, while the finer FFFG is a better choice for small-caliber rifles used for hunting squirrels and rabbits.

If a round ball is used, it should be sized to loosely fit the bore of the rifle. A cloth patch is cut large enough to wrap nearly all the way around the ball. This patch is lubricated by commercial patch lubricant and placed over the muzzle of the rifle. The ball is centered on the patch, and a short starter ramrod is used to force the patched ball several inches into the bore. A full-length ramrod is then used to push the ball down to the breech end. Use the rod to measure the depth of the ball; if it's not seated firmly against the powder, the resulting air space can cause dangerously high pressures when the charge is fired. Elongated minié balls are heavily lubricated and loaded without patches.

With a percussion rifle, the final step is to place a fresh percussion cap against the nipple and lower the hammer to its safety notch. The hammer is drawn back to full cock just before the rifle is fired. To prepare a flintlock for firing, check to see that the piece of flint or pyrite is properly clamped in the hammer dogs and adjusted to strike a spark when it hits the frizzen (the elongated piece of steel the flint strikes against when the hammer falls). Then fill the priming pan with finely granulated black powder, and close the pan cover. When the hammer is fully cocked and the trigger pulled, sparks will fly from the frizzen into the priming pan. When the priming powder is ignited, the flame passes through a hole in the barrel to the main propellant charge inside the bore. As this powder rapidly burns, the gases created force the projectile down and out the bore.

Black-powder shotguns are loaded in much the same way. The big difference is that the

Double-barreled black-powder bird guns let you shoot twice before reloading.

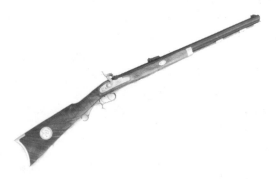

Thompson/Center's Cougar is a modern Hawken replica. This black-powder rifle features stainless steel fittings.

CVA Pennsylvania Long Rifle is a replica of a flint-lock hunting rifle.

Lyman Great Plains rifle is offered in both percussion and flintlock versions. Flintlock rifle is illustrated.

projectile consists of an ounce or so of loose shot in place of a single ball. This necessitates the use of fiber or cardboard wads both under and over the shot charge. A thick fiber wad is first rammed down the bore over the powder charge. Then a measured charge of loose shot is poured down the barrel and a light cardboard wad rammed in over it. This wad holds the shot charge in place and keeps it from running down and out the bore whenever the muzzle is tilted down. These wads can be used dry, or you can lightly lubricate the top wad with commercial lubricant or even saliva. Lubricating the over-the-shot wad helps reduce the buildup of powder fouling in the bore between shots and makes cleaning easier at the end of the day.

Depending on bore size, FFG or coarser FG powder is generally used in shotguns. For 12-gauge guns, 1¼ ounces of loose shot is a reasonably heavy load, while an even ounce is plenty in 20-gauge guns. Powder can be loaded in equal volume; use the same measure to throw both shot and powder charges.

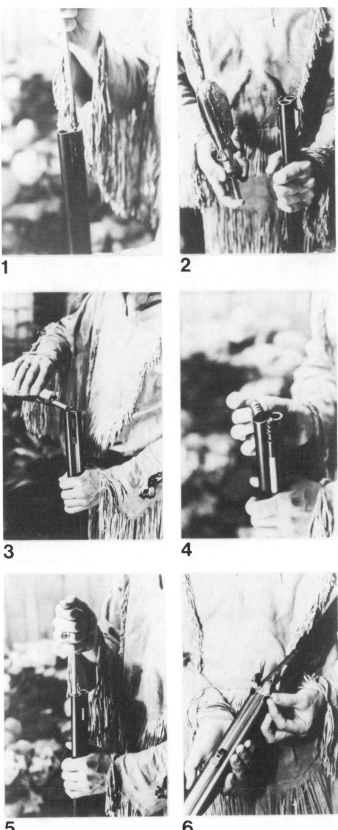

To load a black-powder rifle, first excess oil is swabbed out of the bore (PHOTO 1); then a measured charge of black powder or Pyrodex is poured down the bore (PHOTOS 2 & 3); next, a greased minié ball (or patched round ball) is inserted (PHOTO 4); and the ball is driven all the way down the bore with a ramrod (PHOTO 5). Finally, a percussion cap is placed on the nipple when ready to fire.

Black-powder buffs enjoy the acrid cloud of smoke that masks the target when the guns are fired.

Cleaning Black-powder Guns

To clean a black-powder rifle or shotgun, first disassemble the barrels from the stock. Most muzzle-loading long guns are pinned to the stock by a metal wedge through the forearm. This can be drifted out with a hammer and a block of wood (the wood is placed against the wedge to prevent marring). Then the barrel assembly can be lifted free.

The barrel should then be held muzzle up while hot, soapy water is poured down the bore. The breech end of the barrel should be placed in a bucket or pan to catch the hot water. Scrub the bore using a tight-fitting patch on a cleaning rod, and repeat the soapy, hot-water bath several times. Boiling water should be used, with small chips of bar soap—not detergent—added and stirred until dissolved.

Once the bore has been thoroughly scrubbed, rinse the entire barrel in boiling hot, clean water. If the water is hot enough, the barrel will retain enough heat to dry quickly and thoroughly through evaporation. If the water is too cool, some may remain within the bore or in other hard-to-reach places and cause rusting.

Finally, swab both the bore and the external metal surfaces with a light coat of gun oil. This will guard against later corrosion. The oil within the bore should be swabbed out just before the gun is again loaded for firing. A couple of percussion caps should be placed on the nipple and fired in succession before the first powder charge is poured down the barrel; this will burn out any excess oil from the nipple and firing chamber.

Black powder is highly corrosive, so guns fired with this propellant must be cleaned thoroughly and as soon as possible—certainly no later than the evening after the shooting session takes place.

9

Deer Hunting

Deer hunting is the favorite sport of many million Americans, and the sheer volume of deer rifles, ammunition, sleeping bags, and other equipment sold to these hunters each year is enormous.

In some states, entire communities close down when deer season begins. Schools hold a holiday and businesses shut their doors temporarily to allow everyone the chance to be in the woods on opening morning. Untold tons of venison are consumed each year by the families of successful hunters, and taxidermists do a brisk business mounting trophy racks.

Deer are the largest game many states have to offer, and these animals are eagerly sought coast to coast by nimrods who may plan their entire year around the hunt. Sportsmen travel hundreds, sometimes even thousands of miles to hunt deer. Deer-rich states like Colorado, Utah, and Wyoming are inundated by out-of-state hunters who enrich both state game coffers and the local economy.

There are basically three different kinds of deer hunted in the United States—whitetail, blacktail, and mule deer. They are the most hunted large game animals on this continent.

Whitetail Deer

The whitetail is the smallest of the three and ranges the entire United States, with the exception of a thin belt of country through the central states and a wide strip along the Pacific coast. These deer do not do well in dry country and are scarce or absent in Utah, northern Arizona, southwestern Idaho, and in parts of California, Nevada, Colorado, and other western states.

This species is easily identified by antlers that have all points branching out from the

Deer hunting is the favorite sport of millions of Americans.

main beam, and by the large, broad white tail or "flag." The whitetail is largely a brush-country deer and spends most of its life in thick foliage, marshy country, and brush-bordered open meadows. These deer are also found around farms, orchards, and in heavily timbered areas.

Unlike mule deer, the whitetail doesn't migrate from summer range to winter range but lives within an area of a few square miles. Mule deer are often found in very open country and tend to move into high, rough mountainous or timbered terrain to escape heat, flies, and natural enemies in summer.

Although the whitetail is the smallest of the three species, exceptional bucks weighing 300 pounds have been recorded. Mule deer, on the other hand, are heavier on the average than are whitetail or Columbia blacktail deer. All overlap each other's range to a degree.

Blacktail Deer

The blacktail is a Pacific coast inhabitant and a subspecies of the mule deer, with many of its characteristics. It has the same antler type, even the same stiff-legged bouncing gait, but has a flat tail shaped like that of the whitetail.

Blacktails roam from the Sierra Nevada and Cascade ranges to the coasts of California, Oregon, and Washington, as well as north along the coast of British Columbia and into the southern part of Alaska, where they provide excellent hunting.

In the West, a popular method of hunting blacktails is to hunt in pairs. One hunter works along a ridgetop overlooking a canyon or valley; the other, moving slightly behind, works up from the bottom. Each partner has a chance to see deer spooked by the other.

Mule Deer

Mule deer range over the greater part of the western United States and Canada, as well as south into the upper part of Mexico and Baja California.

The muley has several distinguishing characteristics, and derives its name from its large, mule-like ears. Both mule and blacktail deer have lighter faces than whitetails do, with a dark horseshoe mark on their foreheads. Mule deer have a light patch similar to that found on elk, and a thin white tail with a black tip. The whitetail has the largest tail of the three species, pure white underneath and darker than the body color on the outside. In the summer, these deer have coats of red, yellowish red, or light brown. The fall coat of all three is deep gray brown or olive brown, blending into yellow brown on legs and flanks, with white inside the legs, under the tail, and on the underbelly.

The whitetail ranges throughout most of the United States. Whitetails are generally smaller than mule deer, but 300-pound bucks have been recorded. (MAINE DEPARTMENT OF ECONOMIC DEVELOPMENT)

Mule deer range over the greater part of the western United States and Canada. Look for the buck to follow last in line.

Deer feed most actively at night but do browse off and on throughout the day near their bedding areas.

When deer are on the move, hunting from ambush is the best way to ensure your venison supply.

A freshly used deer trail makes a fine ambush point.

Stalking Deer—Doing It Right

Deer are grazers as well as browsers. They live on grass and small plants in the spring and summer months, feed on brush and acorns in the fall, and, as snow grows deeper, subsist on tips of brush, moss, bark, and the branches and twigs of various trees.

Deer feed most actively at night and bed down during the heat of the day. Consequently, the early hours of dawn and the later part of the afternoon are the most productive times to hunt these animals. In the morning, the deer are on their way to their bedding areas, while by late afternoon they're ready to feed again.

When deer are on the move, the best tactic is to hunt from ambush. Deer have sharp eyesight and spot movement readily. On the other hand, deer are color blind, and a bright-orange-clad hunter can remain virtually invisible to his prey if he'll only sit still. If you can locate a freshly used deer trail that shows heavy movement along it, watching this trail from a nearby vantage point is likely to pay off early and late in the day. Sitting and waiting for a buck to show up also makes excellent sense on the season opener. The woods are most crowded with hunters on the opening day of the season, and their movements will keep deer active all day.

It requires both patience and discipline to sit on a deer stand hour after hour, particularly when the temperature drops below freezing. If you plan to spend a good part of the day sitting motionless on a stand, dress warmly enough to ensure comfort. Wearing several layers of clothing is better than relying on a single, heavy coat or jacket. A coat warm enough to keep you comfortable in the predawn cold will be too hot and heavy after the sun has been up a few hours. And it will be overly burdensome if you decide to try stalking later in the day. If your clothing is in layers, you can simply add or remove garments to suit the temperature and your activity.

Toward midday, most deer will be bedded

When deer bed down for a midday nap, a skillful still hunter can sometimes locate bucks in heavy cover.

down and napping, although some animals will stand and browse periodically. This is the time for you to start moving—but very slowly and carefully. It's possible to walk up a deer in its bed, but it requires a little luck and a fair amount of stalking skill. Remember to always hunt with the wind in your face. That should keep the animal from scenting you before you're in sight. If you hunt with the breeze at your back, the deer will have plenty of advance warning to escape unseen.

The most common mistake deer hunters make is to move too rapidly through the woods. A skillful stalker will take a slow, careful step, then freeze 15 or 20 seconds while he looks for any sign of movement, or for an object that could turn out to be an ear, eye, leg, or any part of a hiding deer. A small pair of binoculars come in handy, even when hunting in heavy brush. These magnifying optical aids can help you distinguish between foliage and animal flesh when a suspicious\ object is sighted.

Your ears also play a vital part when you're

Most hunters move too rapidly when trying to sneak up on deer. A skillful sportsman will freeze 15 or 20 seconds after each step while he looks around him for possible movement or signs.

stationary stands, while the second slowly moves through the woods, using all their stalking skills to get as close as possible to any deer they might run across. The drivers will inevitably push deer ahead of them, and these deer will be concentrating more on the action behind them than on the danger ahead. This gives the stationary hunters lying in wait an excellent chance to score. A fleeing deer who senses trouble both on his backtrail and ahead will sometimes panic and turn around and blunder into one of the other drivers. Both drivers and standers have a good chance to see game within rifle range.

In some areas, whitetail hunters climb trees or elevated stands and wait for unsuspecting deer there. Deer seldom look for danger from above, and their high perches give these sportsmen a commanding view, allowing them to see down through thick brush and timber.

One key to successful hunting is to arrive at the hunting site a full day or more early. This gives you a chance to thoroughly scout the area for fresh deer sign and become reasonably well acquainted with the terrain. Well-used trails can be located, and you'll have time to select likely ambush sites and make sure you can find your way to these areas in predawn darkness. Get your scouting done *before* you begin to hunt, and your chances for success soar.

ghosting through the woods. If you surprise a deer in heavy timber or brush, chances are you'll hear him before you see him. The startled thump of his hooves as he makes his stiff-legged escape may be the only notice you'll have of his presence. If you move quietly enough and stay on the alert, you may hear deer that are moving in your direction, often as they sneak away from another hunter. This gives you an excellent chance to lay a quick ambush, or simply get into good shooting position before the animals step into view.

Whitetails are often hunted by driving, with hunting parties splitting up into two groups. The first group circles on ahead and takes up

Where to Aim to Make a Kill

When shooting at deer, don't make the beginner's mistake of simply shooting at the entire animal. Aim for a particular point on the animal. Some knowledge of deer anatomy is helpful, but the best aiming point on an animal standing broadside is just behind the front shoulder about halfway up the body. This will pierce the lungs and, if the shot goes low, it should shatter the heart, as well. If the shot is a little too far forward, it will break the shoulder and ruin a couple of roasts but will also anchor the game. Take care not to shoot too far *behind* this mark, though, or you may lose a wounded animal. If the animal is facing you,

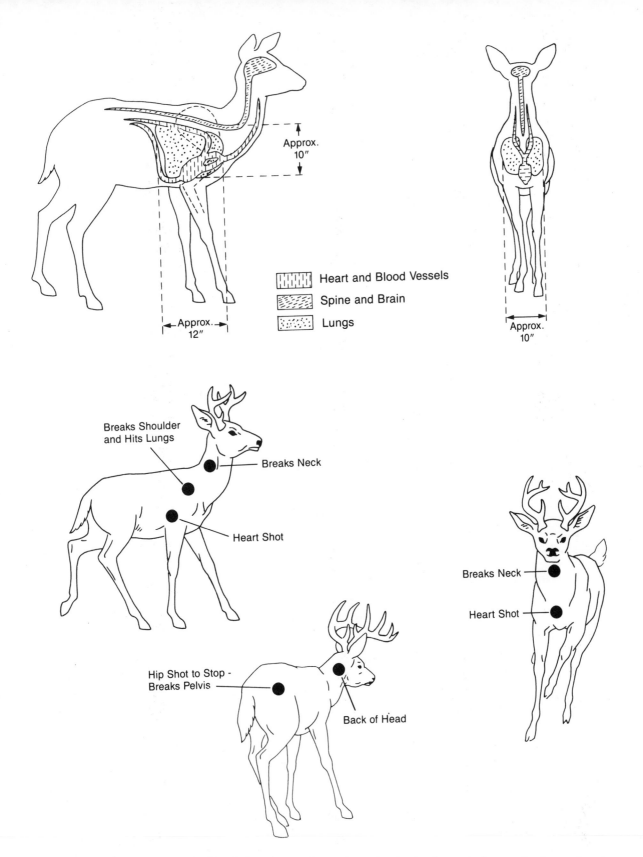

Heart and Blood Vessels
Spine and Brain
Lungs

Approx. 10"

Approx. 12"

Approx. 10"

Breaks Shoulder and Hits Lungs

Breaks Neck

Heart Shot

Breaks Neck

Heart Shot

Hip Shot to Stop - Breaks Pelvis

Back of Head

Don't make the beginner's mistake of shooting at the entire animal; aim for a vital spot: the lungs, heart, spine, or neck. (COURTESY BROWNING)

simply center the sights on its chest. A deer running directly away from you presents a poor target, although a bullet striking the spine will often kill instantly.

Once the animal is down, approach it cautiously. Make sure your rifle is ready for a fol- low-up shot, if this proves necessary. Any wounded animal is dangerous, and the antlers and sharp hooves of a deer can cause serious injury. If the animal's eyes are closed, it could be merely stunned; eyes that are open and beginning to glaze usually indicate death, but

John Rees with his first mule deer buck. Rifle is custom 6mm Remington with fiberglass stock.

even this sign isn't a sure one. Poke the animal with your rifle muzzle or a long stick. If the deer moves at all, shoot it again.

How to Dress a Downed Deer

To ensure good eating, deer must be cleaned immediately after being shot, and the carcass cooled. Some hunters cut the animal's throat as a first step to allow the carcass to bleed. This isn't really necessary; the bullet does enough damage to start the bleeding process, and bleeding continues as the game is dressed.

To dress a downed deer (or any other deer-sized animal), first place the animal on its back, preferably with the head and shoulders slightly uphill. Take a small, sharp hunting knife and make an incision all the way around the anus. This incision should be deep enough to completely separate the rectum from its surrounding tissue. If the game laws require the scrotum to be left in place for later sex identification, cut around the genitals; otherwise, simply cut them off.

Next, insert the knife into the loose belly skin at the front of the pelvis, and slit the belly all the way up to the chest. Be careful not to cut too deeply; if the inside organs are cut, intestinal matter will contaminate the stomach and make the balance of your task more odious. Separate the ribs from the lungs and diaphragm, and reach as far as possible up inside the neck cavity to sever the windpipe. At this point, the loose organs and viscera can be rolled out of the cavity. Save the liver and heart; these are not only edible, but delicious when properly prepared.

If the inside of the body cavity has been contaminated with intestinal matter, use water or snow to wash the cavity out. Otherwise, simply wipe off any excess blood with a clean cloth, or simply allow the carcass to drain. The remaining blood will form a glaze that helps keep the flesh clean.

If a small meat saw or hatchet is available, it's a good idea to cut down the center of the rib cage to expose more meat and speed the cooling process. The body cavity should be

After being dressed, deer should be either cut up and carried or simply dragged to camp or to the nearest access road.

propped open with sticks to aid air circulation. Removing the skin will also facilitate quick cooling, but also makes it harder to keep the meat clean until you've transported the carcass home or to a game processing facility. Sprinkling liberal quantities of black pepper on the exposed flesh helps keep blowflies at bay, but if the animal is to be left hanging in camp the carcass should be sealed in a loose-fitting muslin game bag. A few sticks inside to hold the loose muslin away from the carcass will prevent flies from laying their eggs through the porous cloth.

The dead animal should be left on the ground for only the shortest possible time; otherwise, the side contacting the ground will retain its heat and may begin to spoil. Small

It's important to dress any deer-sized game as soon as possible. This Wyoming antelope will make fine eating, thanks to prompt attention.

deer may be carried out, but be sure to prominently attach some blaze orange cloth to the antlers and/or body to prevent some hunter from taking another shot at it as you tote it through the woods. Larger deer must be dragged to the nearest access road, or butchered and carried out in halves or quarters.

Some hunters insist on removing the scent glands on the lower part of a buck's hind legs. This isn't really necessary, as long as these glands aren't cut or rubbed against the meat during the dressing process. However, care should be taken to remove any hair that may be on the meat after dressing, as this will cause tainting.

If the antlers and head are to be mounted as a trophy of the hunt, the skin must be carefully caped. The skin is slit from a point between the buck's ears, along the top of the neck to the withers. A second cut is made encircling the deer's body from the top of the withers—joining the original cut—down over the shoulders to the bottom of the chest. The hide is then worked forward to the base of the head, and the entire head is cut off just behind the jaw. The flesh should then be salted, and the caped

Dressed deer should be hung well off the ground as quickly as possible to promote cooling. (U.S. FOREST SERVICE, SOUTHWESTERN REGION)

head and horns taken to the taxidermist at the first opportunity. Photographs taken of the deer before caping begins give the taxidermist valuable help in making a lifelike mount.

Safety Considerations

Because there are so many rifle-toting hunters in the woods on opening day of deer season, safety becomes a primary consideration. Never point a gun or rifle at another human—or, for that matter, at anything you don't intend to shoot. It can be highly disconcerting to find yourself staring into the rifle muzzle of another hunter on a far hillside. Some riflemen inexcusably use the magnifying scope sights mounted atop their rifles in place of binoculars to "glass" the terrain. Examining another hunter through your riflescope is simply asking for a shooting accident, even if your rifle's safety is engaged.

Each year, some shooting accidents occur because an overeager rifleman mistakes another hunter for game. For this reason, a certain amount of blaze orange or hunter orange clothing is required wearing for all deer hunters in the woods during the regular rifle season. It's illegal to hunt without such safety attire, which is easily seen even at great distances. Since deer are color blind, the bright orange color doesn't disturb or alarm them.

10

Hunting North American Big Game

While deer remain the favorite target of American riflemen each fall, there is a wide variety of even larger game available. Depending on where you live, or how far you're willing to travel and how much you can spend, you can hunt western elk, moose, black bear, or smaller animals like antelope without crossing any international borders. Cougar are also fair game.

Travel north into Canada or Alaska and you can hunt caribou and grizzlies. If you crave still more adventure, you can stalk the giant Alaskan brown bear. Alaska's moose are also oversize, and make top trophies. And don't forget mountain goats, or Dall and Stone sheep.

Black bear, while nowhere nearly as plentiful as deer, are nearly as widespread. *Ursus americanus* is found in both the eastern and western states, as well as in the states bordering Canada. The bears also appear in several southern states, along the Rockies, and throughout Canada and Alaska.

Hunting with trained dogs is the most productive method, although banned in some states. Spring hunting over bait is also very effective, although this, too, isn't legal in many areas. It pays to check the local game laws before heading for the bear woods.

Hunting Bears

An adult boar blackie generally weighs between 200 and 400 pounds, although much larger specimens have been recorded. Some black bears in Alaska rival inland grizzlies in size, and may weigh 600 pounds or more. Deer rifles ranging from the .30-30 Winchester up to the .270 and .30-06 are adequate for the smaller bears, but a more powerful magnum provides comforting insurance where oversized

While most black bears weigh between 200 and 400 pounds, they grow larger in Alaska. This 7½-foot specimen shot by Robert Brooks is as large as many grizzlies.

bears may be encountered. While grizzlies have the more fearsome reputation, many outdoorsmen are seriously mauled each year by black bears.

To hunt grizzlies, you must travel north into Alaska or British Columbia. Alaskan brown bears, of course, are found only in Alaska, along the coast. These huge carnivores may approach three quarters of a ton in weight and measure ten feet tall when standing upright. The Alaskan brown bear is nothing more than an oversized grizzly; its enormous size is attained through the plentiful, salmon-rich diet available in or near Alaska's coastal areas. Rivaled only by the polar bear in size, the brown bear is North America's most impressive—and most dangerous—trophy.

Hunting either inland grizzlies or Alaskan brown bears requires a guide unless you're a native of that state. Licensed guides are expensive but greatly improve your chances for success. They also provide a necessary safety factor; one of the major functions of a bear guide is to stand ready with a big-bore magnum in case your marksmanship proves faulty or the bear simply requires additional stopping persuasion. Even a heart-shot grizzly can live long enough to cover 100 yards in under 5 seconds and kill you very dead.

Because the big bears are so tenacious of life,

Some Alaskan grizzlies weigh nearly 3/4 ton; they are our largest land-dwelling carnivores. Connie Brooks's .375 H&H Magnum Bighorn rifle evened the odds on this trophy.

conventional hunter wisdom is to use a large, heavy bullet at magnum velocities and shoot for the front shoulder. Breaking either front shoulder is *supposed* to immobilize a grizzly and keep him from charging. The same bullet is likely to damage the lungs and other vital organs. One-shot kills are rare, and grizzly hunters are well advised to keep on shooting as long as there appears to be any life left. Even 1,200-pound brown bears are extremely fast, and if you encounter one at close range you're likely to have time for only one shot. This is another reason it's so comforting to have a steely nerved guide alongside you with his rifle.

The status of the polar bear as a game ani-mal has been changing and remains uncertain. One thing you can be sure of is that white bear hunting will increasingly be exclusively a rich man's sport. Only a very limited number of hunts have taken place in recent memory, although Eskimos still have the right to harvest the great white bear. The nonresident hunter who does get the rare opportunity to hunt po-lar bear will pay dearly for his sport.

When hunting *any* bear—brown, black, or white—unexpectedly encountering a sow with cubs is a situation to be avoided. In most cases it's illegal to kill a female bear with young, and mama bears have explosive tempers and very short fuses. Big boars will eat cubs at every opportunity, so sows are conditioned to viciously defend their young against all comers. They're likely to charge first and question your intentions later.

Because even a small black bear has surprising speed and strength and is so well equipped with an assortment of deadly cutlery, any bear hunt offers at least a small degree of danger. This is one reason bears are so highly regarded as trophies. Hunting the big, northern bears offers first-class adventure at even greater risk. While this risk is very real if you hunt bears in thick cover, most grizzlies are shot on open hillsides at ranges of 200 yards or more. Under these conditions a decent marksman is very safe, particularly with a rifle-toting guide at his elbow.

Stalking Moose

Moose are North America's biggest game, and the world's largest deer. The giant Alaskan or Alaska-Yukon moose stands 7½ feet high at the shoulder and may weigh as much as 1,800 pounds. Its antlers are enormous and may span 6 feet or more. These huge animals are found only in Alaska, the Yukon, the Northwest Territories, and the northwestern part of British Columbia.

The Canadian and northwestern moose are hunted throughout Canada and in Minnesota, while the smaller Shiras moose are found in Montana, Idaho, Wyoming, Utah, and southeastern British Columbia.

Depending on the area, moose season usually begins in August or September. By mid September the rut is under way and bulls lose much of their native caution. At this time they can often be lured within easy rifle range by grunting and by thrashing brush to imitate a rival suitor. Another good ploy is to pour a stream of water from a hat or other makeshift container from chest height into a lake or pond. This mimics the sound of a cow urinating and can be highly effective if there's a love-sick bull in the neighborhood.

At this time of year, moose are unpredictable and may even charge hunters under cer-

Moose are the world's largest deer and North America's biggest game. This British Columbia bull was taken with a .30-06 Colt Sauer rifle.

tain circumstances. Moose are hunted both in watery bogs and in timbered mountains at surprisingly high elevations. These huge deer feed on aquatic plants during spring and summer months, but by the fall hunting season they are usually browsing on willow, birch, aspen, alder, and a variety of other bushes, saplings, or trees.

Moose are not difficult animals to kill in spite of their large size. A .270 or .30-06 makes an adequate choice, although many hunters prefer a 7mm or .300 magnum. The first-time moose hunter is likely to be amazed, if not intimidated, by the formidable butchering task a freshly killed bull presents. Because these animals are so massively heavy and hard to manage once they're down, it's best to avoid shooting them while they're standing in a lake or

Moose can often be lured into bow range during the rut by mimicking the sound of a rival suitor. (BEAR ARCHERY PHOTO)

stream. Dressing out a moose while you're floundering waist-deep in water is a chore to be avoided at any cost.

The moose's enormous nose is a highly efficient scenting tool, but its eyesight is weak and uncertain. Moose are quick to spot movement but may not be immediately alarmed by it. The animals have excellent hearing, and they move surprisingly fast when startled. They make excellent eating when properly cared for.

The Elk

Elk are considerably smaller than moose, but a big bull may reach the half-ton mark.

Even a 700- or 800-pound wapiti is an impressive animal. A mature bull that sports six full points on each side of its rocking-chair rack is a prized trophy; seven-point antlers occur, but rarely.

While elk were once common throughout the United States, huntable populations now exist in only the western and mountain states. Hunters have the best chance to bag elk in Wyoming, Idaho, Colorado, Montana, and Washington, although New Mexico, Oregon, and Utah are also good bets. Elk can be hunted in Canada, too. Hunting seasons usually begin in September or October. Whistling or bugling is effective early in the season while the rut is

Elk are likely to be shot at long range. This band moving along ridgeline is within good rifle shot.

under way. Both lone bulls and harem bulls are likely to respond to a high, whistled challenge, and it's possible to lure a trophy into easy rifle range if the calling is skillfully done. The bugling of an elk is easy to reproduce, and there are a number of commercial elk whistles on the market. However, a novice shouldn't attempt any calling until he's heard an authentic elk whistle or taken lessons from an experienced bugler. Calling can work any time, but it is most effective early and late in the day.

The best tactics for hunting elk consist of walking or riding the high country, then stopping to glass the meadows below with a good set of binoculars. A spotting scope comes in handy for evaluating trophies in advance. During the mating season, you can often locate elk by listening for their challenges. A bugled reply may cause the bull to start looking for *you*.

When glassing for elk, take care to keep out of sight. Don't walk across a skyline or make too much movement. Elk have excellent vision and are easily alarmed when the woods are full of hunters. They also have keen ears and noses. If you're hunting in company, driving can be effective. Part of the hunters should take up stationary stands downwind of a likely canyon or valley, while the drivers should move with the wind at their backs, allowing their scent to move the animals ahead of them. So warned, the elk are more likely to trot slowly away; if startled, they break into a flat-out gallop and are capable of running at thirty-five miles an hour. A galloping elk makes a very difficult target.

Elk are likely to be shot at relatively long range—200 or 300 yards—so flat-shooting rifles are required. A .270, 7mm, or .30-06 makes a fine choice, although many sportsmen prefer the 7mm Remington or .300 Winchester magnum. The 8mm Remington and .338 Winchester magnums are more powerful than absolutely necessary but are also popular among serious elk hunters. Heavy 150-grain bullets are recommended for the 7mm and .270 calibers, while most .30-caliber elk loads feature 180-grain bullets.

Elk are very big animals to the beginner who's hunted nothing larger than deer, and a hunter without a horse faces a tough task getting the carcass back to civilization. It's the lucky hunter who manages to drop his elk near a logging road; most nimrods aren't nearly that fortunate. A good, sharp knife and a small meat saw are musts if the animal is to be quartered for packing out on foot.

Caribou are considerably smaller than elk but offer equally impressive antlers.

Going After Caribou

Caribou are considerably smaller than elk, but they offer antlers that can be equally impressive. A large Osborn or mountain bull may weigh 600 pounds, but the other subspecies are generally smaller. These animals are hunted in Alaska and Canada, which makes them exotic trophies for most United States sportsmen. Caribou are normally found in the high wilderness country, although the Barren Ground variety migrate long distances through both mountain passes and lowland tundra. If you can arrange to be on the migration path when the herd passes through, they appear in large numbers. At other times, lone bulls or small groups of animals can be hunted. Woodland caribou are fond of the open forest and tundra, while the Osborn variety are usually found above timberline. These animals feed early in the day and bed down on high, windy slopes or patches of cooling snow during the warm afternoon.

Caribou are very agile and fast. Sometimes they allow hunters to approach within easy rifle range. They're remarkably curious animals and can sometimes be lured even closer by a handkerchief-waving sportsman. If the hunter isn't scented, a nearsighted bull is as likely to wander closer to investigate as bolt when he first notices an intruder. Caribou are relatively fragile animals for their size, and any deer rifle in the 7mm or .270 class is adequate medicine.

Bagging Mountain Sheep and Mountain Goats

While Rocky Mountain and desert bighorns are still hunted in a few western states, most sheep hunters concentrate on the Dall and stone variety found in Alaska, the Yukon, and some parts of Canada. The Stone sheep of British Columbia are relatively rare and are becoming increasingly expensive to hunt because of high license costs. Fortunately, Dall sheep are more plentiful, and an Alaskan hunt for these animals isn't prohibitively costly. Dall sheep aren't large animals—few scale more than 200 pounds—but a full curl set of ram horns ranks among the most desirable of hunting trophies. Sheep country is both high and rugged, and hunters need to be in top physical shape to handle it. Good binoculars of 9X or 10X are needed to scout for sheep, and a 25X or 30X spotting scope is a must for evaluating distant trophies.

Mountain goats are also hunted primarily in Alaska and Canada, although there are still fair numbers of these animals in Montana,

Mountain sheep make superb trophies. They can still be hunted in a few western states but most sheep hunters travel north to Canada or Alaska. (OREGON GAME COMMISSION PHOTO)

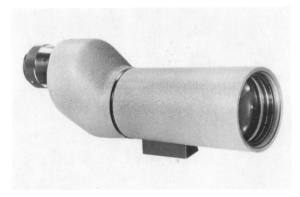

Spotting scopes are a "must" for judging distant sheep trophies. Bushnell Stalker is a compact, lightweight spotting scope designed specifically for hunting.

Washington, and Idaho. A few goats also exist in other states where transplanting has been successful. Goats are hunted in the same high, craggy terrain sheep prefer, and they make the same rugged requirements on the sportsman. Hunting begins in August or September, depending on the area. Both nannies and billies have horns, but the male goat's headgear is usually the more impressive trophy. Any horns more than 9 inches long make an excellent head for mounting.

Goats prefer country that appears nearly vertical, and they like to graze on the new grass that sprouts from recent slide areas. They're also browsers and eat twigs and buds.

Mountain goats are hunted in the same high, craggy terrain that sheep prefer and make the same rugged requirements on the sportsman. (BEAR ARCHERY PHOTO)

Both goats and sheep can be hunted with any flat shooting rifle with sufficient punch for distant kills. The .270 is a longtime favorite, while the 7mm and .300 magnums are superb for this kind of work.

Where the Antelope Reign

American pronghorn, or antelope, aren't "big game" animals in the strictest sense—it takes a big buck to top 130 pounds—but these fleet-footed animals are highly popular among serious hunters, and the bucks' lyre-like racks make prized trophies. Huntable populations are found in several western states, but Wyoming is widely acclaimed as the place to go for

this kind of sport. The Cowboy state has so many pronghorn, or "goats," as they're locally called, that they present a serious problem to ranchers. These animals are so plentiful that you're likely to see more antelope grazing along the roadside than cattle. Montana also hosts numerous antelope, but they're found on grasslands and sagebrush plains throughout the West and north into Canada.

Pronghorn have excellent vision, with eyesight estimated the equal of a hunter's aided by 8X binoculars. They've been clocked at speeds over 50 miles per hour and sometimes can't resist racing alongside a speeding truck or car, then turning in front of it as they pull ahead.

Because they have such keen eyesight, it's almost impossible to sneak up on a resting herd unless you can put a low rise or some

American pronghorn aren't "big-game" animals in the strictest sense, but they're highly prized among serious hunters.

undetected. When the animals bed down for their midday siesta, they're likely to stay in the same area for several hours. This gives you plenty of time to crawl within good rifle range —200 yards or less, if at all possible. Many hunters bang away at animals 500 yards distant; this results in wounded animals that escape to later die. The most challenging part of the hunt is sneaking to within sure shooting range; roadhunters miss most of the real fun.

Midway into the season, it can be profitable to explore broken country well away from the nearest roads on foot. After antelope are shot at a few times from motorized bands of hunters, they often seek sanctuary in relatively roadless terrain.

Any flat-shooting deer rifle is adequate for antelope, but the .243, 6mm Remington, .25-

Grizzly tracks! The Alaskan grizzly offers top adventure to the American big-game hunter.

other solid cover between you and the animals. Antelope are most active in the morning and late afternoon hours and tend to bed down in the middle of the day. A bedded-down band is hard to spot; they simply seem to disappear as they sink to their bellies in the deep sage. The best way to hunt these animals is to drive the back roads in a pickup truck and use high-powered binoculars and spotting scopes to examine each herd you spy in the distance. A real trophy buck will sport heavy, massive-looking antlers with points that curve markedly toward each other. A good, mature buck will have horns measuring 13 or 14 inches in length, while anything over 15 inches is a real trophy.

Once you've located an animal worth stalking, use your binoculars to help plan your approach. Look for low hills, depressions, or ravines that could allow you to approach

Hunting big game often means traveling to the North country, and using horses for transportation once you arrive.

06, and .270 Winchester are favorite choices. Once down, these animals should be very promptly dressed and processed. Desert temperatures can be uncomfortably high in the early fall, and pronghorn meat can spoil rapidly.

Cougar—the Big Chase

Cougar are also a bit undersized for "big game" classification but make for an exciting chase. Like black bears, these felines are hunted with dog packs, while the hunters follow behind listening to the music of the hounds. When the cat finally trees, the dogs are tied up safely nearby, while the hunter either takes photographs or shoots the animal. Most hound men prefer to hold their dogs and let the cat escape to run again another day. The real sport is found in running and treeing the animal; shooting is anticlimactic.

Cougar, or mountain lion, are best hunted in the western states sporting the largest population of these cats: Utah, Idaho, Colorado, and Nevada. The animals are also fairly numerous in parts of Arizona and New Mexico, as well as sections of Washington and Oregon. Without a knowledgeable guide and a pack of trained hounds, hunter success is virtually nil.

11

Hunting Small Game

Jackrabbits and cottontails are the most popular game animals in America, and there are a host of other diminutive beasts that get their share of gunning pressure. Squirrels are prime targets in many parts of the country, and raccoons and opossums offer fine sport wherever they're found.

Varmint hunters imitate the distress calls of rabbits to lure hungry coyotes, bobcats, and foxes close enough to shoot. They also test their long-range marksmanship on marmots, ground squirrels, and other rodents. Deer and other, larger game may be more glamorous, but small-game hunting is where the real action is.

Most small game can be hunted within a short drive of home. Squirrels and cottontails usually thrive near farmlands, though they can sometimes be found without leaving the city limits. High-powered rifles and other costly gear aren't needed to hunt these popular animals; an inexpensive .22 rimfire or single-shot shotgun will do the trick. Most big-game hunters cut their shooting teeth by hunting rabbits and other small animals found close to home. Teenage nimrods have always taken great delight in a squirrel or rabbit hunt, where they learn the safety and marksmanship habits that will serve them through life. What's more, very few sportsmen ever outgrow the small-game habit. Even after safaris to Alaska, Africa, and other distant parts in search of exotic or dangerous game, most globe-trotting nimrods continue to delight in a morning cottontail hunt or jackrabbit shoot.

Hunting Rabbits

Rabbit hunting is divided into several different categories. The cottontail rabbit is widely

Rifles or shotguns are used to hunt rabbits.

bounding, zigzagging gait that makes the animal very hard to hit.

A lone hunter or a pair of hunters can score by walking through likely cover and kicking rabbits out. If the animals aren't too alarmed, they'll often stop and sit after running a short distance. This gives the .22 rifleman his opportunity.

Cottontails are welcome table fare, though the possibility of tularemia, or rabbit fever, does exist. This disease is rare but can be transmitted through handling when the rabbits are dressed and cleaned prior to cooking. To be on the safe side, it's wise for a hunter to wear disposable rubber gloves when dressing any rabbit or hare. Thorough cooking makes the meat safe to eat.

The varying hare, or snowshoe rabbit, is larger than the cottontail, provides fine sport,

distributed throughout the United States and is the variety most often hunted. Either shotguns or .22 rifles are used, and a fair number of rabbits are taken with handguns and even arrows. These rabbits are usually found in areas where both food and concealment are nearby; they like brushpiles, weed-choked ditches, bramble patches, and woodpiles.

Beagles and other dogs are often used to hunt cottontails. Hunters make use of the fact that fleeing rabbits often run in a wide circle when chased, and eventually wind up somewhere near the starting point. When a dog starts a rabbit from its form, or hide, the smart sportsman simply stands and waits for the rabbit to circle back, then drops it with his shotgun. Scatterguns are preferred for this kind of sport when the rabbit presents only a fast-moving target. In addition to running along at 20 miles per hour, the cottontail has a

Jackrabbits provide year-round sport for small-game hunters in many states.

A jackrabbit makes a high-kicking getaway. Hitting a fleeing jack requires both skill and luck.

A lone hunter can score on rabbits by walking through likely cover and kicking them out.

and is equally good to eat. These animals are found in mountainous areas, usually in the northern parts of the country, although they appear as far south as West Virginia in the East, and Colorado and California in the West. *Lepus americanus* wears a brown coat in summer, turns mottled brown-and-white in the fall, and is totally white during the winter months. An all-white rabbit surrounded by snow has only its coal-black eyes to betray its position. Otherwise it blends perfectly with its white environment.

When dogs are used, these powder-puff hares are easily located and started from their forms. This gives gunners a fast-moving target best suited for a spreading pattern of shotshell pellets. Sportsmen who hunt without canine help will pass up many rabbits that remain motionless and depend on camouflage for safety. It takes practice and a sharp eye to detect a snowshoe rabbit against a snowbank. Once located, such hares are easy marks for rimfire riflemen.

While cottontails and snowshoes make fine eating, jackrabbit flesh is tough and stringy. These animals are edible but not prized by gourmets. Jackrabbits are found in many states, though they are most numerous and common west of the Mississippi River. The

chief identifying characteristics of the jack are its long ears, long legs, and large size. Jackrabbits weigh between 3½ and 7 pounds and can make kangaroo leaps spanning 20 feet when pressed.

Unlike cottontails, jackrabbits don't circle back when chased. If chased by dogs, these hares may quickly put 2 or 3 miles behind them in a more or less straight line. For this reason, jacks are very seldom hunted with dogs. These rabbits are fleet enough to outrun most canines, and if they flush (jump from cover) far enough ahead with a dog at their heels, the hunter will never get a shot.

When heavily hunted, jackrabbits will typi-

Snowshoe rabbits, or varying hares, turn all-white in winter months, make fine eating.

Rimfire .22 autoloaders make fine rabbit and squirrel rifles. FROM LEFT: Mossberg, Remington, Marlin, and Ruger .22s.

cally flush well out of shotgun range and often start moving ahead of the hunters while they're still 100 yards or more distant. Many western nimrods use flat-shooting centerfire rifles when hunting desert jacks. This armament makes 200-plus-yard kills possible and provides excellent shooting practice. The most popular firearm used for hunting jackrabbits is the .22 rimfire rifle, which is useful out to 75 or 100 yards. The .22 rimfire magnum is an even better choice; it offers greater killing power and an additional 30 yards or so of extra range.

The most productive method of hunting jackrabbits is for a group of sportsmen to walk in line 15 or 20 yards apart. This tactic flushes most of the rabbits ahead of the hunters, although a few of the animals may freeze in place to let the line pass by. Like most other hares and rabbits, jackrabbits are plentiful or relatively scarce, depending on an 8- to 10-year cycle. When the population is booming, shooting can be fast-paced in the right locations. In many states jackrabbits aren't afforded "game animal" status and can be hunted year-round without restriction.

Squirrels

Squirrels are widely hunted throughout the United States. They make fine eating. There are several varieties of tree squirrels, but the

Marmots are popular targets of long-range varmint hunters.

Ground squirrels make tiny targets for varmint-hunting riflemen and handgunners.

most popular among sportsmen are the eastern gray *(Sciurus carolinensis)* and the fox squirrels *(S. niger).* Hunting seasons vary greatly from state to state, and regulations should be carefully checked before the sportsman heads for the squirrel woods. Squirrels are very fond of nuts, wild cherries, pinecone seeds, mulberries, corn, and other tasty foods. In winter they also eat buds and immature twigs.

Nut shells and husks found on stumps or littering the area under hardwood trees are sure signs of squirrel activity. Squirrels are very playful, highly communicative animals and can often be located by their high-pitched chittering. Squirrels become very wary under hunting pressure and soon learn to keep the solid bulk of a tree trunk between themselves and any intruder. A pair of hunters working in tandem can circumvent this ploy; one stands stationary, rifle or shotgun at the ready, while the other works his way around to the far side of the tree. The bushy-tail will watch the moving hunter and maneuver to keep the tree trunk as a shield. Inevitably, this will give the motionless gunner at least one clear shot as the animal moves slowly around the tree.

Both shotguns and rifles are used, with .22 rimfires generally favored by most squirrel addicts. Real marksmen shoot for the head, which both enhances the sport and damages little edible meat. Lone hunters should sit quietly and wait for the action to resume after walking into a squirrel hotspot. After 5 or 10 minutes have elapsed, the hunter can often coax hiding animals into view by rapidly tapping the edge of a coin against the flat of another to mimic feeding chatter. Commercial squirrel calls are also available.

Hunters of bobcats, foxes, and coyotes similarly use calls to lure these predators within shooting range. These animals are largely nocturnal, but may respond to a well-blown call at any time of day. The hours of dawn and dusk are usually productive, while some hunters call at night with the aid of a headlamp, where legal. Bobcats and coyotes typically circle downwind and approach the caller cautiously, keeping alert for danger signs. Foxes tend to be less careful; one reason they hurry toward a call may be to beat larger predators in the area to the dinner table.

The commercial calls sold to attract hungry

Some varmint hunters call fur-bearing predators within range by imitating the squall of an injured rabbit.

Heavy-barreled .22 centerfires with high-powered scopes are used for long-range varmint shooting. Note size of 5-shot group, indicating good varmint-shooting accuracy.

carnivores imitate a rabbit in distress, and there are records available for the hunter who has never heard these sounds. Varmint callers should wear camouflage clothing and face makeup and sit very quietly when calling. The calls should begin very loudly, then gradually taper off as though the rabbit is weakening. Most beginners tend to overcall. A half-dozen series of diminishing squalls are enough; the hunter should wait at least 10 minutes before trying again. After a half hour or so of calling from the same spot, the hunter should move to a new site a mile or more away and start over.

Rodent-hunting riflemen get lots of marksmanship practice when they spend an afternoon gunning for marmots, ground squirrels, and similar small varmints at ranges up to 400 yards away. Fast-stepping .22 centerfires in accurate bolt rifles get the nod here, as do 8X, 10X, 12X, or 16X scope sights. These animals congregate in large colonies and a hunter who

finds the right site can enjoy all the shooting he wants without moving more than a few yards. Varminting is a year-round sport, and in some states a hunting license isn't required to shoot rodents, small predators, jackrabbits, and other animals that haven't been accorded game status.

Raccoons

The raccoon can be found in most wooded areas of North America. This 2- to 3-foot-long animal prefers living in trees or hollow stumps, generally near water for easy feeding and washing. Raccoons like rough terrain with thick briars, brushy thickets, creeks, marshes, and sandy beaches.

When cornered, a raccoon will fight anything, including man and dog. Woe to the dog that meets a big male in the water. The raccoon will climb on the dog's back, dig in his claws, and stick like a burr until the dog drowns. The raccoon is a nocturnal animal and is usually hunted in late evening. Hunts last on through the night, sometimes not ending until nearly daybreak. Coonhounds are used to scent, chase, and tree the animal; the *coup de grâce* is administered with a .22 rifle or handgun when the hunters arrive on the scene.

Opossums

The opossum principally inhabits the southeastern part of the country but has spread as far west as California, Oregon, Washington, and north to Michigan.

Like the raccoon, this slow-moving, ratlike creature isn't particular about what he eats. He's thoroughly omnivorous; small mammals, frogs, bird eggs, insects, fruit, or whatever it can scrounge, make up its diet. The opossum inhabits the same type of terrain that raccoons favor. This hairless-tailed marsupial is usually found in wooded areas, swamps, and along streams or lake shores; it typically seeks shelter in abandoned dens of other animals. Hollow trees, woodpiles, drainpipes, and other natural or man-made sanctuaries also serve the opossum as home.

Again, dogs are used to hunt these night-roaming beasts in much the same way raccoons are treed. As a matter of fact, it's not uncommon for a coonhound to bay an occasional possum, although this delights few coon-hunting purists.

A number of other animals qualify as small game, but some are limited to fairly restricted locations. The javelina offers popular sport in parts of Texas, New Mexico, and Arizona and is all but unknown elsewhere in this country. Idaho has the pygmy rabbit, while other areas have their own unique fauna. Wherever you live you can find animals to hunt, and wherever hunting exists, adventure follows.

12

Upland Bird Hunting

Upland bird hunting is popular for many reasons. It takes fast reflexes and excellent coordination to bring down a fast-flying bird on the wing. There's not a gunner alive who can predict the erratic flight of the woodcock, and the rocketing pheasant or bursting covey of quail can tax the finest shooting skills. Upland gunning is always a challenge.

Many a startled hunter has stood and watched a just-flushed bird zoom away without even raising his shotgun. No matter how much bird-hunting experience you've had, you always know that a certain number of grouse, pheasants, or quail will fly when you least expect it. How well you do will heavily depend on how quickly you can recover from the surprise, and what kind of gun-handling reflexes you have.

One of the joys of upland hunting is working behind a well-trained dog. The hunter lucky enough to have four-legged help will invariably be more successful than dogless nimrods. A good dog will smell hiding birds that most two-legged hunters would miss, and it will untangle confusing scent trails laid down by the wily ringneck in its efforts to escape. Once the bird is run to ground, a pointer will keep it frozen in place until the gunner arrives. After the bird is downed, the dog will then retrieve it for his master. If the bird is only wounded, the dog will quickly trail it and prevent its escape. Because a good dog all but eliminates birds lost to wounding, the canine partner is a real aid to game conservation.

It's possible to enjoy good upland sport without using dogs. Dogless gunners must move more slowly and carefully when working through likely cover; otherwise, they'll walk right past many hiding birds. Lone hunters should stop and circle back every now and then to unnerve ring-necked pheasants that may be lying low nearby. Small groups of

One of the joys of upland hunting is working behind a well-trained dog. Dogs add greatly to hunter success. (SAVAGE ARMS PHOTO)

hunters can work more efficiently than a single gunner can, particularly when dogs aren't available.

Quail

Quail may well be the most popular upland game bird in the country. More than forty states harbor one or more species, and quail offer the longest of all game bird seasons.

The bobwhite ranges from central New England down into the deep South, and from the Atlantic coast throughout the midwestern states. Scaled and desert quail are found throughout the Southwest, and valley and mountain quail inhabit the area ranging from the state of Washington south into Mexico.

Valley quail are worthy competitors of the celebrated bobwhite. Valley quail stay in place well when pointed by a dog, and some say these birds are more alert and make sportier shooting.

Mountain quail, sometimes called mountain partridges, are the largest of the quail group, weighing from one half to three quarters of a pound and measuring 12 inches in length. The average bobwhite is about 9 inches long.

The primary difference among the three types of mountain quail is in minor color variation. The birds all range between 11 and 12 inches in length and have similar habits.

Although these birds inhabit the mountain slopes, they are found in a widely diversified range along the Pacific coast and live from the humid valleys of the California coast to the plains of Oregon, from chaparral brush thickets to the banks of rushing streams.

The northern bird is found on the Cascade and Sierra Nevada ranges from Oregon south to Nevada and west to California. The central bird inhabits the high coastal mountains as well as the semi-arid sections of Oregon south to California. The southern mountain quail is distributed along the mountains of Southern California into the mountainous sections of Baja, California.

The scaled quail is a bird of the southwestern United States and northwestern Mexico. The behavior patterns of this desert bird and the bobwhite are similar, since the quail is characteristically a bird of habit. When undisturbed, it repeats its feeding time and place and roosting hours in the same routine manner each day. It feeds on the seeds of mesquite, cactus, sage, and weeds and, near agricultural areas, wheat, corn, oats, and other grain. It likes fruits from orchards and wild desert berries from juniper, desert hackberry, mistletoe, barrel cactus, and other desert plants. Its animal food consists mostly of grasshoppers and other insects.

The Gambel or desert quail is one of several species of western upland quail. It is a handsome, good-eating bird that has its own dedicated following of sportsmen. These desert birds are talkative when feeding. Their most common call is a shrill "chu-chaaa, chu-chaaa" uttered by the cock and audible at considerable distance. Both male and female birds use the scatter call "quirrt, quirrt." Like the bobwhite, the valley quail signals with the familiar "cha-qua-qua." Mountain quail have more of a shrill call than do the smaller birds.

When hunting any species of quail, look for areas where their natural food is abundant. Quail food consists of wild fruits, berries, weed seeds, grain, and insects. Quail will also raid cultured orchards and berry patches.

When hunting in new or unfamiliar areas, contact the local wildlife conservation officer to learn the best quail hot spots. If you can't locate a game officer, ask a few farmers or ranchers where to shoot. If they have quail on their property, always ask permission to hunt in advance.

Dogs give the quail hunter a big advantage as they point and retrieve, but if the dogs aren't well trained, they can spoil your hunt by ranging too far in advance and flushing game out of range. Desert quail would rather run than fly, and even some good bird dogs will flush them before the gunner can get in a shot. Bird dogs are a necessity in dense, tight cover; otherwise, too many downed and crippled birds are lost.

In the Southwest, rugged four-wheel-drive vehicles are often used to provide access to vast sections of desert in the search for birds. Some hunters outfit their dogs with soft leather bootees to keep them from becoming sore-footed in cactus areas. Saddle horses are also used, with the dogs foraging ahead or trailing the riders.

Some scattergunners will admit to jangled nerves when quail have rocketed from under their feet. Those short, stubby wings beat a whirring tattoo that can startle and thrill in the same instant. The bird disappears like magic if you aren't prepared.

Why are quail so difficult to hit? For one thing, they're temperamental. Quail will get up practically under your feet and fly straight at you, behind you, sail straight away, suddenly climb or dive. They can be hit, but it takes steady nerves, practice, and a little bit of luck.

First, you must train yourself to remain calm when that ball of feathered dynamite explodes in your face, only to cannonball away brush-high and quickly out of sight. Be prepared by expecting birds to flush any moment when you've located a covey; have your shotgun at the ready, with your thumb on the safety. Many easy shots have been missed simply because the shooter was taken by surprise. The tyro often makes the mistake of shooting at the entire covey instead of picking out a single bird and staying with it.

Quail are generally shot at close range. This calls for a light, fast-handling shotgun with open chokes using size 6, 7½, or 8 shot. For thick brushy areas, most hunters prefer the dense pattern provided by 8s or 9s.

Pheasants

Pheasants are also highly popular targets for upland gunners. Natives of Asia, these birds were imported as early as the eighteenth century by George Washington and other wealthy sportsmen. Those early efforts failed to establish the Chinese ringneck in this country, but a small flock sent to Oregon in 1881 flourished and in a matter of decades these colorful birds were successfully introduced in a dozen other states.

Today the ringneck is found in most states, although it does poorly in the South. Huntable populations are in the northern half of the country and are most numerous in the grain states of the Midwest. South Dakota, Iowa, and Nebraska are particularly noted as prime pheasant producers, although hunting is good throughout the Midwest. California, Oregon, Washington, and Idaho also offer fair pheasant gunning.

Pheasants love corn and wheat stubble and can be found almost anywhere there's a bit of cover on harvested farmland. Fencelines, overgrown ditchbanks, standing cornfields, rows of milo—all provide sanctuary for the Chinese

Pheasants are highly popular upland gunning targets. These Asian imports are widely distributed throughout most of the United States.

Happy hunter with rooster taken in an Idaho beet field. Ringnecks are a favorite of upland gunners.

cacklebird. A pheasant doesn't need much cover to make itself invisible; it can sink from sight behind a few spindly sprigs of wheat, and disappear in a field that looks totally barren of hiding places.

Dogs are a tremendous asset in hunting pheasants. A good dog will not only find and flush the game but also retrieve it. A lone hunter has to work harder for his birds than a small party of nimrods will, regardless of the cover, but a well-trained dog gives any upland gunner a big edge.

Hunting large fields of wheat or standing corn is best done with several hunters and a couple of dogs. Before the dogs and the bulk of the hunters enter one end of an extensive cornfield, two or more gunners should circle and station themselves at the far end, 60 or 70 yards apart if the field is considerably wider than that. Otherwise the stoppers should post themselves at the corners. Very large fields should be hunted in strips, with hunters moving slowly no more than 10 or 15 yards apart. With wider spacing the birds are likely to double back through the line or simply freeze until the hunters pass by.

When the drivers get within 150 yards of the stoppers posted at the end of the field, care should be taken to avoid shooting in another

Dogs are a tremendous asset in hunting pheasants. A good dog will not only find and flush the game, but also retrieve it.

hunter's direction. Birdshot pellets aren't lethal at that distance, but a stray pellet could damage an eye. For the same reason, low-angle shots should be avoided. Typically, a few birds will flush before the moving line of drivers, but 90 percent of the action will take place at the very end of the field, when the driven ringnecks find themselves trapped between the opposing groups of hunters. Hunt such fields to the very end, and be prepared for fast shooting. When hunting in standing corn, extra precautions are necessary to avoid shooting accidents. The drivers should keep close track of the hunters on either side and make sure the line stays straight. Again, avoid shooting at low-angle birds unless you're positive the shot pattern won't endanger another hunter. Standing cornfields can be highly productive, but re-

duced visibility makes them more dangerous to hunt than open ground.

Dense thickets and brushy woodlands also provide good cover, particularly after the first few hours of opening day. Similarly, pheasants often seek sanctuary in marshes and swamps, where cover is heavier than in the surrounding terrain.

A good time to look for ringnecks is at sunup, when they come in from the open meadows and grain stubbles where they have roosted overnight to assemble along the roadsides and replenish their crops with gravel. Where sunrise shooting is legal, country roads and lanes are good places to find pheasants.

Shortly after daybreak, the birds slip into grain fields where they fill their craws and then head for hedgerows, brushy ditches, or other cover to rest during the heat of the day. Once their midday dusting and resting period is over, the birds head again for the grainfields or other nearby food. Toward sunset, they again fill their crops with gravel, then roost far out in a stubble field or somewhere else they feel secure.

A modified or improved-cylinder choked 12-, 16-, or 20-gauge gun works best for most pheasant hunting, although full choke may be needed late in the season when the birds are flushing wild. Field or express loads of No. 5, 6, or 7½ shot are recommended.

Chukar Partridges

Chukar partridges were imported from India. These birds are chiefly hunted in the western and Rocky Mountain states where the climate is relatively arid. They are often found in rough, rocky country along canyon rims and foothills. On steep sidehills it's folly to chase a flock uphill, as the birds run effortlessly up slopes that will quickly wind both hunter and dog. Hunting downhill is the best tactic, but birds fly this same direction when flushed, which puts them quickly out of range.

Grouse-sized, these birds are easily distinguished by their red legs, gray coat, and scalloped wings. Their peculiar "chu-a-chuk,

chuk-a-chuk" call can be heard over a mile on a still morning. The chukar's flesh is mostly white and very tasty.

Before hunting chukars, check with local game officials to see where populations have been planted. Any good quail dog will work well on chukar. These birds can be hunted effectively without four-legged help, but dogs save a lot of leg work in running down cripples or retrieving distant kills.

Chukars, like quail, travel in coveys and if pinned down by a dog before they start running will flush like quail. Hunting singles after a covey breaks is more difficult than with other birds, since they scatter over a longer distance.

Grouse

There are several different kinds of grouse hunted in this country. The ruffed grouse is a popular target that enjoys wide distribution, particularly through the northern half of the United States, up through Canada, and as far north as Alaska.

The Canadian or spruce grouse lives in northern New England, New York, Michigan, and Minnesota, westward to Alaska and Canada, and along the northern border of the states. The Franklin, blue, dusky, and sooty grouse inhabit the pine and fir forests of the West. The sharptail is largely confined to the Northwest but is also found in plains country along with the pinnated grouse, or "prairie chicken." The sage grouse is the largest of the species and is found in the sagebrush deserts of the West.

Hungarian partridges are widely distributed throughout the wheat belts of both Canada and the United States and are occasionally found in some eastern states.

Again, checking with wildlife conservation officers is the best way to locate local grouse populations. Remember that grouse are seldom far from water. Look for them near small creeks and springs. Grouse also like man-made trails and roads where they can get the gravel needed to grind their food. They also like midday dust baths, and if you can find a heavily

Sage grouse are large, desert-dwelling birds of the West. They are usually found near water.

used dusting ground you know you're in good grouse country. The grouse is one upland bird that can be hunted without the services of a dog. These birds often hold tight in low-level cover, allowing a hunter to come within a few feet before flushing. In flight the grouse is erratic, dipping and dodging to put bushes, trees, and other natural cover between itself and the gunner. Downed birds may be located from the sound of the rapid fluttering of their wings —a trait of dying grouse. Unhit birds seldom fly far and will generally sit tight until flushed again.

Doves

The mourning dove is the smallest of our upland game birds and is the least man-shy. This bird breeds in every state except Hawaii and Alaska and migrates south in the fall. Doves generally water in the morning and late afternoon, and feed in grain fields and sunflower patches. They often perch along fences and power lines and can also be spotted in low wheat stubble and other feeding sites. Doves can be shot as they fly from feeding to roosting areas. Standing quietly alongside a line of trees can be productive. Shooting over a water hole in late morning or afternoon provides excellent gunning if birds are in the area, or you can walk doubles and singles up from grainfields or wherever you can see birds working.

Because doves migrate, an area that furnishes top gunning one day can be almost barren of birds the next. Doves have little tolerance for bad weather, and a sudden rainy or cold spell can move them out in a hurry. These birds are hunted under Federal migratory game-bird rules, and guns must be plugged so the magazine will hold no more than two shots. With another load chambered, that lets you shoot three times before reloading is necessary.

Doves are hard to hit but easy to kill. Improved-cylinder or modified choked guns are best, with field loads of 7½ or 8 shot. In the South, the white-winged dove is a popular target. These are hunted along creek beds and flushed like grouse or pheasants. They can also be shot over waterholes or as they fly in to feed.

Band-tailed pigeons are hunted along the west coast. All these birds tend to concentrate along the southern tier of states in late fall, and they furnish fantastic shooting for hunters who travel into Mexico during midwinter.

Wild Turkeys

Wild turkeys constitute our largest upland game bird, with mature gobblers weighing as much as 20 pounds and sometimes even more. Turkeys are now hunted in some thirty-five states, with both spring and fall seasons available, depending on local regulations.

In addition to being our largest game bird, the turkey is also the wariest. It takes a fair amount of both skill and luck to be successful on a weekend hunt; consequently, a big tom turkey is highly regarded as a hunting trophy. Hunters should carefully scout areas in advance of the season to determine where the birds are feeding and roosting. Turkeys generally roost in tall trees located high on a ridge or in some other elevated area where unobstructed flight is possible. Roosting sites can be identified in daytime by the droppings and fallen feathers that are found under roost trees.

Once feeding and roosting areas are found, the best strategy is to position yourself somewhere along the path the birds will take on their way to breakfast. Camouflaged clothing is a must, and the hunter must sit or lie perfectly still. The turkey has superb hearing and sees equally well. For this reason, it's next to

Mourning doves offer fast shooting when they migrate south every fall. They're hard to hit but easy to kill.

Side-by-side double makes a fast-handling gun for upland game.

impossible to stalk within shotgun range of these birds.

In the spring, many turkeys are taken by sportsmen who use some kind of call to imitate a yelping hen. Calling is most effective from a ridge or other high ground. Wood or slate calling boxes are sold commercially, as are diaphragm calls the hunter operates with his mouth. Calls can also be effective when a flock has scattered, as the birds are gregarious and will soon try to regather.

Both rifles and shotguns are used to hunt turkeys. Large-bore shotguns are recommended, with full-choked 10- and 12-gauge guns leading the list. Magnum or express loads of size 2, 4, or 5 shot are recommended. Riflemen prefer .22 centerfires like the .22

Hornet, .222 or .223 Remington, fitted with a good 4X scope. Riflemen should aim for the juncture of the turkey's neck with the body.

Woodcock

Woodcock, in contrast, are very small birds, averaging between 5½ and 7 ounces in weight. These birds have very long bills, large heads, and eyes set well back on the head. The prime breeding areas are in the northeastern states, and the birds migrate south for the winter. Hunting seasons vary, depending on when the birds will be in the area.

Woodcock, or timberdoodle, eat insects, berries, and some seeds, but worms form their staple diet. Accordingly, the best hunting habitat

Upland game birds should be drawn and cleaned soon after shooting for best table fare.

For hunting doves or waterfowl, make sure the magazine of your shotgun is plugged to limit its capacity to three shots.

will feature dark, soft earth where worms are easily reached, along with trees for cover and concealment. The birds are often found in alder thickets, as well as in birch or pine. They also feed in boggy pastures and orchards, where the ground is rich and soft enough to attract earthworms.

Dogs make things easier for the woodcock hunter but aren't absolutely necessary for success. Moving slowly on an erratic or zigzag course is a good way to flush birds, with or without a dog.

Light, open-choked shotguns throwing size 8 or 9 shot work best in most woodcock cover. Timberdoodle aren't hard to kill, although their dodging flight makes them very hard to connect with.

13

Waterfowling: Hunting Ducks and Geese

Almost all ducks and geese breed north of the Canadian border—many in Alaska and the Northwest Territories. There are four great waterfowl flyways: the Pacific, Central, Mississippi, and Atlantic. When the breeding season is over and the young ducks and geese have attained their flying feathers, they raft up and head down these main flightways in the fall and head south for the winter. It is one of nature's greatest spectacles for both bird watcher and hunter.

Know Your Ducks and Geese

Before you ever enter the field to hunt, you should visit a nearby waterfowl refuge or pond in your city park so you will know what the various species of ducks and geese look like and how each species sounds and acts. This will be a good time to invest in a good duck or goose call. Listen to their visiting and feeding chatter and try to imitate it very carefully. In time you will be able to call them properly to your hunting blind when you go afield. It might pay to purchase a waterfowl record so you can practice at home. Olt's game-calling records for ducks, geese, squirrels, foxes, and other game sell for a few dollars each and are well worth the money. It is also advisable to have the little booklet "Ducks at a Distance," a waterfowl identification guide published by the U.S. Fish and Wildlife Service, Department of the Interior. Write to the U.S. Government Printing Office, Washington, D.C. 20402.

With over sixty species of waterfowl, it is no wonder sportsmen become confused at times. It is *important* to recognize the various species, as some are protected and some hardly edible. Learn to recognize the birds on the wing, to avoid taking birds you don't want. Otherwise

Whistling swans are legal game in some western states. These are big birds that require magnum loads of large shot.

you may shoot an illegal bird and have to spend an expensive visit to the courtroom. After you have followed the above instructions, go out with an experienced waterfowl hunter.

Watch the maneuvers of a flock in the air; this will help indicate the species. Mallards, pintails, and widgeons form loose groups; teals and shovelers flash by in small bunches; mergansers often appear in single file; canvasbacks shift from waving lines to temporary V's; redheads "boil up" in short flights from one end of a lake to the other. In closer view, individual silhouettes can show large heads or small, broad bills or narrow, fat bodies or slender,

long tails or short ones. Experienced observers also identify ducks from their wingbeats; they may be fast or slow, short rapid flutters or long strokes. Depending on light conditions as they close the range, color areas can be positive. In early morning and toward evening before the sky lights up they may not appear in their true colors, but their size and location will help identify them. The sound of wings can be as important as that of the voice. The pinions of goldeneyes whistle in flight; the swish of wood ducks is different from the steady rush of canvasbacks. Not all ducks quack; many whistle, squeal, or grunt. Knowing the species of ducks

Latex rubber Deeks are self-inflating and take up little space in a hunting coat.

and geese can be a rewarding experience for the scattergunner, and when extra birds of a certain species are permitted in the bag, sportsmen who know their waterfowl come out ahead of the game with a more abundant bag limit. If you shoot birds you cannot identify, you may meet up with a game warden and spend a day in court. *Remember,* habitat, action, color, shape, and voice all help distinguish one species from another. It is also well to recognize the brighter plumage of the male bird.

Two Groups of Ducks

Ducks are more or less split up into two groups: puddle ducks and diving ducks. Puddle ducks are typically birds of fresh water, shallow marshes, and rivers rather than large lakes and bays. They are good divers but usually feed by dappling or tipping up rather than by submerging. There are various ways of distinguishing to which group a duck belongs. For example, puddle ducks leap straight up into the air when taking off, while divers skim along the surface. Another difference is the hind toe of these two groups. The diving duck has a broad lobe which acts as a rudder; the puddle duck's is smaller. All birds and waterfowl will attempt to take off into the wind.

Any ducks feeding in croplands will likely be puddle ducks, for most of this group are surefooted and can walk and run well on land. Their food is mostly vegetable; there is nothing finer than grain-fed mallards, pintails, or corn-fattened wood ducks. The puddlers ride higher in the water than the divers and launch themselves directly upward when rising, whether on land or water.

Types of Shooting

Generally there are three types of waterfowl shooting for either ducks or geese: jump shooting, pass shooting, and decoy shooting. Let's take them in order:

Jump Shooting

Jump shooting is popular across Canada and the United States, especially in pothole or prairie country. Jump shooting, practiced mostly by natives of the area, involves stalking quietly through marsh cover and creeping up on small ponds, sloughs, and creeks where single ducks or small flocks are hiding and flushing ahead of the gun. When they rise above the rushes and tules, the shooting takes place. The trick is to approach with the wind, since the birds will head into the wind and fly straight up and away. When jump shooting from a scull boat or other craft, the reverse is often best. The sneak boat can get closer to the sitting or rafted ducks, so the gunner usually approaches upwind, taking ducks as they fly straight away from the boater.

Another form of jump shooting is from a canoe or sneak boat when the ducks are sitting tight in the bulrushes. One hunter rows or paddles quietly among the rushes while the other shoots from the bow.

Geese stack up as they prepare to land and feed. A snow-camouflaged gunner waits.

Pass Shooting

In pass shooting you locate a spot where birds pass over early in the morning and where they return in late afternoon to raft up in protective waters for the night. The birds will travel this route daily as they trade back and forth from one body of water to another or from one grain field to another

Once the pass route is located, the hunter conceals himself in whatever cover is available and waits until birds come over. This, however, is shooting at maximum ranges, and substantial leads with magnum loads of No. 4, 5, or 6 shot through full choke barrels are in order.

In other instances, shooting is done over water or from a point of land projecting out into a bay or river. A boat or a retriever is needed to recover birds that have been shot and fallen into the water, especially so if there is any current or wind drift. Too many birds are shot over water with no means to recover them.

Decoy Shooting

Shooting over decoys is by far the most popular form of waterfowl hunting, and generally is the most successful. If possible, the hunter

A hunter calls ducks in over decoys. Reeds provide a natural blind, and camouflaged clothing helps break up the gunner's outline.

first builds his blind well in advance of opening day. When the season opens, he arrives ahead of shooting time so that his decoy stool is "set" in the water before waterfowl start to take wing for their feeding ground.

The type of blind that is built depends on the area and terrain. Often the hunter will improvise on the spot and take advantage of nearby material. Another consideration is the species of waterfowl being hunted. For example, black ducks require carefully constructed blinds that are well camouflaged and do not loom up on the landscape, while other puddle ducks and divers will usually come into decoys in front of a blind not so carefully designed.

The best waterfowl blinds are those that stay in the same place year after year and become part of the natural landscape. New blinds often startle the birds. Permanent blinds are usually found on private property and at waterfowl clubs and are used for such shallow-water species as blacks, mallards, widgeon, teal, etc., because the areas these birds work can be easily determined. To build a permanent blind in a good location, the hunter must find where the birds will pass close enough to a point of land, a curve in the riverbank, or the edge of a lake.

Temporary blinds, like permanent ones, range widely in size, shape, and comfort. Sometimes it is possible to improvise a blind by utilizing nearby natural cover, such as thick patches of reeds, brush, rocks, corn shocks, or

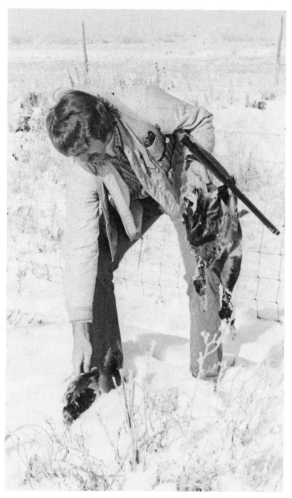

Jump-shooting ducks makes a fine winter sport. No decoys are required for this type of shooting.

Geese are large birds that require a solid hit with heavy loads of large shot to down. Ithaca Mag 10 10-gauge autoloader makes top goose medicine.

wind-thrown trees. If the ground is soft, a two-foot pit can be dug and pieces of chicken-fence wire three feet wide can be used around the upper edge laced with reeds. Inexpensive camouflage netting can be used to cover the wire. The blind should be arranged so that the waiting hunter has his back to the wind if possible. This allows him to face waterfowl coming in naturally against the wind.

One of the greatest handicaps to the blind

shooter is the character who has to walk around outside the blind to keep warm or can't keep his head down inside and his face concealed from approaching birds.

If it is necessary during a quiet period to pick up downed birds, take your scattergun with you. If you get caught out in the open and ducks are approaching, freeze, and they may still come within range.

Stubble Shooting with Decoys

Stubble shooting is practiced on the prairie, mainly in western Canada and parts of the U.S. Middle West where mallards and pintails

Decoys are the key to shooting ducks over water. The blind is nearby.

feed in harvested stubble grain fields. From some high point, try to observe the line of flight as the birds trade back and forth from water to field. Drive until you locate this feeding ground. Once located, do not disturb; al-low them to leave by themselves. Next, contact the landowner for permission to hunt. If per-mission is granted, the hunter can take advan-tage of the natural cover or dig a well-con-cealed pit blind. If the breeze is coming from

A good retriever will find crippled waterfowl that might otherwise be lost.

your left, the decoys should be placed in scattered feeding positions upwind of the blind, with the right-hand edge of the spread opposite the pit and about 20 to 30 feet off. A dozen or so blocks should be about right. (When shooting on small marsh ponds, half a dozen decoys is sufficient for puddle ducks.) Get comfortable and wait until the next feeding period when birds are coming in or passing over. Don't open fire on them until they are 25 to 35 yards off. Ducks generally feed twice: right after daybreak and again from late afternoon until they raft up in the middle of open water or hide out in the tules and marsh rushes for protection from their enemies. In late season and during stormy weather, the birds feed continuously, flying back and forth between field and protective water.

Types of Decoys and How to Use Them

Duck and goose decoys come in many sizes, species, materials, and prices. Wooden, molded Styrofoam, cork, and plastic decoys are excellent but bulky. Latex rubber Deeks weigh less than 6 ounces apiece. By holding the Deek 6 or 8 inches above the water, it will inflate the instant you drop it on the water and deflate in-

stantly when you lift it off. When deflated for carrying or storage, the anchor is dropped inside and is tucked in the head. A ring in the stem and ballast prevents unnatural side-rolling.

Another popular decoy is the folding cardboard silhouette. These are lifelike and designed for field use, and can be obtained with adjustable heads, upright and in feeding positions.

Setting the Stool

Duck hunting is always at its best when the weather is at its worst, and if there is any wind to speak of, ducks will invariably land upwind. If the wind is blowing from the right of your blind, set the decoys to the left of center so the landing area will not be too far to the right. Reverse the setup if the wind is opposite.

How many decoys should be used in a stool? For large bodies of water, the more the better. A dozen decoys suffice for puddle ducks, but for open-water ducks (divers and skimmers) experienced gunners may place as many as 100 to 200 decoys in a "set."

Puddle ducks and divers decoy in different ways. The divers usually pass over decoys before landing, while puddle ducks either pitch right into the middle or land outside the stool and swim in.

All these things should be taken into consideration when setting the stool. If it's divers you are after on bays and inlets, remember that they overshoot, so set your decoys slightly downwind from your hideout. For puddle ducks, set your decoys so that they have landing room right in front of your blind—15 to 25 yards out. Often a half-dozen decoys are sufficient for a small pothole lake, and a dozen or more for larger lakes and river sandbar shooting.

There are many ways to make a set. Two methods that have proved successful are the V and J patterns. Wind is vitally important in planning a big water layout. Where puddle ducks can get in and out of a tight landing area, even on a crosswind approach, the faster

In waterfowling areas where the point system is in effect, species identification is a must before you shoot.

divers will always make their landing approach upwind and usually well out, and need a larger area to skid down into. When using these time-tested sets, place the V with the opening downwind and the point in front of the blind for puddlers. The "hook" of the J is suitable for large sets for divers.

In grain fields, or "stubble shooting," decoys are spread out as though feeding, and the ducks are shot as they pass over or come in to land.

Tips to Remember

Don't mix diver and puddle duck decoys in a set. Six to eighteen blocks are sufficient for puddle ducks as mentioned earlier; don't crowd them. Divers will come into large, close spreads of three or four dozen or more decoys if conditions appear normal. Black ducks are the most wary, but sometimes a few goose decoys will allay their fears, and they might draw in a stray goose or two to add to your bag. Set the goose decoys upwind from your spread and not too close. Don't set your duck decoys closer to your blind than 20 yards.

Estimating Range

An odd decoy set out in front of your blind at 40 yards will give you a marker for estimating range. If you shoot with a companion, in the case of a right-handed shooter, he will naturally shoot only from the center front of the blind and to his right, and the left-hander from center to his left for safety reasons. Try to visualize how ducks will look to the shooter at various ranges.

A hunter wades back to the blind with the kill. Decoys lure ducks into gunning range.

Leading Waterfowl

When hunting waterfowl, or any other species of bird, one of the most important things is to *remember to lead the first bird picked as a target and stay with it until you drop it.* Don't just haphazardly shoot into a flock of birds hoping to make a hit. You will probably just blast a hole in the sky or wound birds that will fly away and die.

In most areas, the first waterfowl to arrive are small ducks which decoy easily. These are bagged with light loads if the shooter leads the bird properly. As the season advances, the big puddlers and divers come in on the north wind, and heavier or magnum loads are indicated. For these, it is suggested you use No. 4, 5, or 6 shot. Here again, an adjustable choke device will give good results and versatility.

What Kills Ducks

What kills waterfowl and upland game birds is a combination of pattern density and shot penetration. Since most waterfowl are shot within 30 to 40 yards, there is little need for a heavy, long-barreled shotgun. The smart waterfowler will wait until ducks are within upland game-bird range before shooting. Under these circumstances birds can be taken with lightweight, short-barreled upland guns with modified choke with the above-mentioned shot size. When shooting over decoys or when jump shooting along creeks and potholes, the long-barreled, heavy duck gun becomes a handicap to many shooters. That is why more and more lightweight upland game 12-gauge guns are used today in duck blinds. In turn, many more waterfowlers are becoming better

Hunting over decoys provides fast gunning action when the birds are flying well.

marksmen, since they have to concentrate on identifying ducks and geese. That means that the gunner must allow the birds to approach or attract them into closer range. Naturally, you will have to be more careful with camouflage, with blind building, and even with calling.

Geese

To simplify the classification of geese, waterfowlers generally divide the geese of this continent into three groups: the gray, the white, and the blue. Under the gray classification come the Canadas and their subdivisions, such as cackling, Hutchins, lesser Canada, and western Canada. The white geese comprise the greater snow goose, which is confined to the east coast, and the lesser snow, sometimes called wavey, which occurs throughout most of our western states and Mexico. The Ross's goose is another "whitey," and the smallest of the North American geese; it spends most of its winters in the Sacramento Valley rice field areas of California. The blue goose is medium-sized and is almost always associated with lesser snow geese on land and water, on breeding grounds, on migration, and on the wintering grounds. The blues probably are the most plentiful of all geese. These birds favor the Mississippi flyway and head from their Hudson Bay summer range almost directly to the Louisiana marshes. Added to these are the Brant from the cold Arctic regions. This coastal salt-water goose, about the size of a cackling goose, uses both the Pacific and Atlantic flyways.

The Largest Goose

The largest and most important goose is the Canadian, often referred to as the Canadian honker, which ranges from Alaska to Mexico. This bird is the prize of all waterfowlers and flies in large V formations or long "strings" and back into V formation again. One can hear its cry, "eaur-awk, eaur-awk," for nearly a mile or more. These large birds mate for life. When one is shot down, the mate may hang around until it too is killed.

White camouflage hid author Rees when hunting in snow. This duck was fooled.

How to Hunt Geese

In goose hunting, knowledge of the bird's habits is vital to success. Besides stalking, pass, and jump shooting, the methods in hunting geese of all species include the use of all sorts of blinds and goose decoys. Sneak boats are used to hunt geese at times, and to tend offshore blinds. Boats are used to recover crippled and dead birds.

When geese arrive from the north, they tend to settle down upon coastal marshes and inland prairies from Maine to California and from Washington to Florida to spend the winter months. They rest at night on protective waters and fly out at the crack of dawn to feed in grain fields and tidal marshes.

In the early part of the season, geese are content to graze lightly on waste grain of winter rye or wheat and eelgrass in the tidal flats. Later they tend to feed on harvested leavings of corn, milo, cane, barley, and wheat. At such

times they settle down in certain fields and feed there twice daily, just before sunup and again in late afternoon

In hunting these wily birds, you must first locate their feeding grounds. They will fly from 20 to 40 miles to stubble grain fields time and again until they are spooked out by heavy hunting, or until they pass on to another field where feed is more abundant.

Stubble Fields

Reconnoiter the stubble grain fields and look for goose tracks, droppings, and feathers. Usually they will be found in the low spots in fields where moisture has gathered. A pair of binoculars are helpful when watching where geese light. Once a feeding ground is located, wait until the birds have fed and left the area before you build your pit blind. Geese are creatures of habit and will come back to feed where they left off.

Since the grain fields will be on private property, you will have to seek permission from the owner to dig goose pits or even hunt the property. To keep up good public relations with a rancher, you will have to respect his property, fences, gates, stock, and unharvested crops. All too often, a few thoughtless hunters will leave litter: empty shells, bottles, and lunch papers. Sometimes they forget to fill in the goose pits, making extra work for the rancher. You cannot blame some wheat ranchers for posting their land against hunting. If permission is granted to hunt, perhaps the owner would appreciate a goose for his dinner too. Find out when you quit for the day—perhaps he will invite you and your party back again.

Geese are smart and watchful. Unless forced by strong winds, they will not fly near thick brush patches, shocked corn, or other obstructions that might conceal an enemy. If they do fly over obstructions, it will generally be high and wide. They like open fields where they can watch from all directions. Here is where a well-concealed pit blind is a *must*.

The Goose Blind

The wind has much to do with where you place your blind and goose decoys. Geese never jam up in a tight bunch when they put up for the night, but when ready to take off, they go in a tight bunch until they form in a long string and then go into a more or less V formation. They tend to bunch up in the same manner when frightened off a field.

Some hunters never dig a pit blind, but just use a shallow depression where they place an air mattress or pad on a piece of old gray canvas or a weathered piece of burlap 8 or 9 feet long and 3 or 4 feet wide. They then cover themselves with a somewhat larger piece of camouflage netting or other dull-colored material. This in turn is covered irregularly with field straw and chaff collected nearby. The straw should be picked so that you do not leave bare spots that the cagey birds will no-

tice. All footprints leading to the blind should be erased. This can be accomplished by brushing the tracks out with a handful of straw. When doing this, avoid leaving telltale straight streaks in the snow or on the bare ground. Do the job irregularly or the sharp-eyed birds will edge off. Hide all fresh dirt signs the same way by scattering them and covering them with field litter. Pit blinds should be dug deep enough for concealment when sitting, but with sufficient room for shooting. When using either type of blind, place it where geese left off feeding the day before.

Goose Decoys

Wind has much to do with the proper placing of decoys. The honkers tend to alight short of feeding geese or goose stools. Thus the spread should be scattered loosely within 15 to 25 yards of the pit blind on calm mornings; right between the hunters when the wind is 8 to 16 miles per hour, and as much as 40 to 50 yards upwind on really rough windy days. If you have some decoys with adjustable heads, it is a good idea to position several decoys with their heads down as though feeding, and at least one with its neck straight up, simulating the sentinel bird which always remains watchfully on guard while its companions eat. On water, you will need a minimum of twenty to thirty or more decoys. You can get by on land with more or less the same number, although larger spreads are always more productive.

Stalking Geese

The Canadian honker and other geese are hunted in a variety of ways, depending on the locality. In Canada and our midwestern grain states, they are hunted from wheat fields and goose pits and, along the Mississippi and other flyways, from pits dug in sandbars. On the great sand barrier reefs of our coastal states, they are hunted from pits, brushpiles, and floating blinds.

Geese are exceptionally difficult to stalk in ponds and potholes. They are usually situated so they can observe all directions and are generally out of shotgun range. However, they are more easily stalked from the curving bank of a river. The idea is to spot them as they light on the water, allow some twenty minutes or more to elapse, then creep and crawl within your gun range. Be especially careful not to make any noise or cause the brush to sway if there isn't any wind to make the movement look natural.

A full-grown Canadian honker is a big bird and looks enormous to waterfowlers who have shot only ducks, cacklers, or blues. He appears to be coming in slowly but is actually cutting the air much faster than the less-experienced hunter thinks. Deceptively, geese really move faster in normal flight, despite their slow wingbeat, than do puddle ducks.

Brant and Other Coastal Geese

To shoot these restless birds you have to get near them, and that isn't always easy unless you are a good hand with blind construction and are subtle in setting brant stools.

Tides are important in taking brant in coastal areas. When the tide is high, all the eelgrass, the brant's favorite food, is covered. Then the birds sit it out in the middle of a large bay until the tide recedes and the first areas of eelgrass begin to show above the surface of the falling water. Between flights, the decoys, silhouettes, and floaters have to be moved out farther in the shallow water. One thing brant gunners don't do often enough is move the decoys out to keep up with the falling tide. Brant won't come to decoys that are left high and dry on muddy tidal flats.

When any species of bird is hunted over deep water like this, you need a boat or a well-trained retriever. With a falling tide or an offshore wind it doesn't take long for a downed bird to drift out of wader reach.

Waterfowl Boats

It is possible to hunt ducks and geese without using a boat. Nevertheless, boats of one sort or another play a prominent role in waterfowl hunting. Hunting boats come in various sizes, shapes, weights, and seaworthiness. They may be lightweight car-toppers, canoes, blunt-nosed scows, johnboats, dories, skiffs, or decked-over scull or sneak boats. For big waters, where wind, wave, and current are strong, a more seaworthy craft like the dory is safer. In this case, the boat should be equipped with an outboard motor if you are unable to row against a strong outgoing tide or strong offshore wind. The motor is to be used only in case of emergency, since waterfowl may not be hunted from a powerboat. The motor should be stopped and tilted up on arriving at the shooting area and not used until you head for shore.

Which Shotguns to Use

For pass shooting at geese, magnum 12- and 10-gauge guns provide the extra reach often needed for high-flying birds. Full or modified choked barrels are best, as the shot pattern needs to be concentrated enough at 40 or even 50 yards to bring down a big gander. Long-range shots require BBs or 2's, while 4's provide better patterns out to 40 yards or so. Patterns will be less dense with BBs and 2's, but these heavy pellets retain sufficient energy to penetrate and kill out to 50 yards or so if the bird is properly centered.

Some waterfowl areas require hunters to use steel (actually, soft iron) shot only. Check your local regulations for this possibility before you leave home. Because steel (iron) is less dense than lead, pellets one size larger should be used to provide comparable performance. If you normally use lead 2's on geese, you should substitute 1's or BB-sized pellets when using steel shot.

While duck hunters typically use No. 4, 5, or 6 lead shot, they switch to 2's and 4's when gunning in steel shot areas. Steel pellet-loaded shotshells are more expensive than standard lead-shot-loaded shells, and they're not quite as effective at extended range.

When hunting over decoys, modified or im-

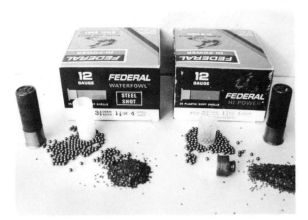

Steel shot is required for gunning some waterfowl areas. Be sure to check local regulations in advance.

proved-cylinder chokes will provide the kind of patterns needed. This is true for hunting either ducks or geese. If you intend to use a single choke constriction for all your waterfowl hunting, modified choke is likely the best compromise. Twenty-gauge guns throwing 1 1/8 or 1 1/4 ounces of shot are fine for hunting over decoys or pass shooting at medium range, but smaller 28 and .410-gauge guns don't throw enough shot to be truly effective.

Whistling swans are hunted on a limited basis in some western states. These large birds are generally shot over water after being attracted by decoys. Goose guns and loads are required for hunting swans.

Since all waterfowl are migratory, they are hunted under Federal rules. Guns must be plugged to hold no more than three rounds, including the load in the chamber. Individual states set their own waterfowling seasons, but season dates must fall within Federally approved calendar limits. Season lengths and bag limits may change annually to reflect the strength of the waterfowl population.

14

Hunting Safety, Manners, and Ethics

Every year a number of sportsmen are killed or wounded while hunting. Most accidents are caused by the careless handling of firearms. Everyone who shoots or hunts should be familiar with the following "Ten Commandments of Firearm Safety":

1. Treat every gun as if it was loaded.

2. Watch that muzzle. Don't let it wander —ever.

3. Open the action of any gun as soon as you pick it up. Then check to see that there is no ammunition in the firing chamber.

4. Be sure the bore is clear of obstructions before firing. Anything that slows or impedes the flight of the projectile as it travels down the bore can cause dangerously high pressures that could damage both the gun and the shooter.

5. Unload the firearm when not in use. Never take a loaded gun into a car or a house.

6. Be sure of your target and backstop. Make certain you're shooting at game and not another hunter. If there's the slightest doubt, *don't shoot.* If you miss, make sure you know where the bullet will travel. Never endanger another person.

7. Never point a gun at anything you don't intend to shoot. If you never point your firearm in an unsafe direction, you'll never have a shooting accident.

8. Don't shoot at a hard, flat surface or water, which may cause ricochets.

9. Store guns and ammunition separately, and beyond the reach of children or untrained adults.

10. Never mix gunpowder and alcohol. If you must drink, wait until the end of the day when the guns are unloaded and put away.

Always obey game laws and respect the rights of property owners. The game law violator is a thief. The hunter who kills more than

Watch that muzzle! Always keep firearms pointed in a safe direction and treat every gun as if it was loaded.

Unload firearms when not in use. Never take a loaded gun into a car or house.

Be sure of your target and backstop. Make certain you're shooting at game and not another hunter.

his legal limit, shoots game out of season, illegally hunts after dark with the aid of spotlights, or shoots edible game and leaves it to rot is no sportsman. Anyone observing an illegal kill should report it to local wildlife conservation officers, along with a description of the violators, their vehicle license number, and any

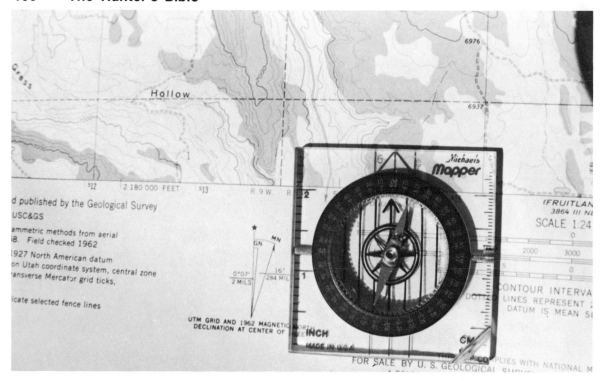

Always carry a compass and a map when hunting unfamiliar wilderness areas. Know how to use them.

Use your map to orient yourself often when you're in unfamiliar country. Follow this precaution and you'll never be lost.

Always carry a supply of matches in a waterproof container when hunting. They could save your life.

Commercial fire starters will let you build a warming fire under almost any conditions.

other information that may prove helpful in bringing the poachers to justice. A direct confrontation may not be advisable, and could prove dangerous. Simply report what information you can safely obtain by observation and leave the matter in the hands of the law.

Whenever you plan to hunt on private land or cross over it to reach your hunting site, always obtain written permission in advance. Then be sure to respect the landowner's property. Close gates behind you, leave fences intact, don't leave unsightly litter, and never shoot near buildings or livestock. Every year more private land is permanently closed to hunting, simply because a few sportsmen angered landowners by impolite or unsportsmanlike conduct. Be considerate.

When hunting in forest or wilderness areas, be equally as conscientious in avoiding litter. Bury all your garbage, or pack it out with you. When you leave a campsite, destroy all evidence of your stay. Dismantle the ring of rocks you used to enclose the campfire, and do everything possible to return the area to its original pristine state. Don't cut down trees. Green wood is almost impossible to burn; use dead, fallen branches as firewood.

From a safety point of view, you should carry a map and a compass when hunting wil-

derness areas you're not thoroughly familiar with. Remember to refer to both compass and map periodically throughout the day to keep yourself oriented. If you haven't been keeping track of your position in relation to camp by taking compass readings regularly, that compass will do you little good when you realize you're lost. With it, you'll be able to keep walking in a straight line rather than circling in your tracks (a common phenomenon among the disoriented), but you'll have little idea which direction will lead you to camp or to safety.

Always carry a supply of matches in a waterproof container, or waterproof/windproof matches, or a disposable butane lighter whenever you're afield. The ability to build a fire is your most important concern when lost in the wilds. A fire will keep you warm and cheerful at night, and it can be seen for long distances. In daytime, creating smoke by placing green boughs on a fire is an effective means of signaling your position to searchers. If you're not confident in your backcountry firemaking skills, carry along a commercial fire starter. These fire-building aids are available in compressed block, loose tinder, or tubed jelly form and can be relied on to get a fire started under all but the worst conditions.

If you don't have a pretty good—make that

Waterproof/windproof matches are excellent hunting accessories.

very good—idea of which direction to walk to lead you to a road, to camp, or to some other sanctuary or form of civilization, your best bet is to stay put until help arrives. Whenever you travel into wilderness country to hunt or hike, you should always notify someone trustworthy of exactly where you'll be going and when you expect to return. When you're twenty-four hours overdue, that friend should immediately contact the local sheriff or some other authority to initiate rescue efforts. This step is important. If no one misses you or knows when you're supposed to return from your hunt, rescue efforts will be greatly delayed.

If at all possible, spend a few days familiarizing yourself with any area you intend to hunt. Note prominent landmarks and any roads in the area, then try not to wander too far afield when hunting begins.

Finally, learn to care for and savor the game you kill. Animals and game birds should be dressed out immediately and allowed to cool. The carcasses should then be kept in a cool, dry place and protected from flies and other insects until you can transport the meat to your home freezer. Wild game provides a rare taste treat and should never be wasted.

Appendix 1

Where to write for hunting information. Game regulations and hunting area maps can be requested without charge from the Game or Wildlife Conservation Departments of any state:

ALABAMA: Dept. of Conservation and Natural Resources, 64 N. Union St., Montgomery, AL 36130

ALASKA: Dept. of Fish and Game, Subport Bldg., Juneau, AK 99801

ARIZONA: Game and Fish Dept., 2222 W. Greenway Rd., Phoenix, AZ 85023

ARKANSAS: Arkansas Game and Fish Commission, 2 Natural Resources Dr., Little Rock, AR 72205

CALIFORNIA: Dept. of Fish and Game, 1416 Ninth St., Sacramento, CA 95814

COLORADO: Division of Wildlife, 6060 Broadway, Denver, CO 80216

CONNECTICUT: Wildlife Unit, Dept. of Environmental Protection, State Office Bldg., 165 Capitol Ave., Hartford, CT 06115

DELAWARE: Division of Fish and Wildlife, Tatnall Bldg., P.O. Box 1401, Dover, DE 19901

FLORIDA: Game and Fresh Water Fish Commission, 620 S. Meridian St., Tallahassee, FL 32301

GEORGIA: Dept. of Natural Resources, Game and Fish Division, 270 Washington St. SW, Atlanta, GA 30334

HAWAII: Fish and Game Division, Dept. of Land and Natural Resources, 1179 Punchbowl St., Honolulu, HA 96813

IDAHO: Fish and Game Dept., 600 S. Walnut, Box 25, Boise, ID 83707

ILLINOIS: Department of Conservation, 605 Stratton Office Bldg., Springfield, IL 62706

INDIANA: Department of Natural Resources, 607 State Office Bldg., Indianapolis, IN 46204

IOWA: Conservation Commission, Wallace State Office Bldg., Des Moines, IA 50319

KANSAS: Kansas Fish and Game Commission, RR 2, Box 54A, Pratt, KS 67124

KENTUCKY: Dept. of Fish and Wildlife Resources, Arnold L. Mitchell Bldg., 1 Game Farm Rd., Frankfort, KY 40601

LOUISIANA: Louisiana Dept. of Wildlife and Fisheries, 400 Royal St., New Orleans, LA 70130

MAINE: Dept. of Inland Fisheries and Wildlife, 284 State St., Station 41, Augusta, ME 04333

MARYLAND: Dept. of Natural Resources, Maryland Wildlife Administration, Tawes State Office Bldg., Annapolis, MD 21401

MASSACHUSETTS: Dept. of Fisheries, Wildlife and Recreational Vehicles, 100 Cambridge St., Boston, MA 02202

MICHIGAN: Dept. of Natural Resources, Wildlife Division, Box 30028, Lansing, MI 48909

MINNESOTA: Dept. of Natural Resources, Wildlife Section, Box 7, 300 Centennial Bldg., St. Paul, MN 55155

MISSISSIPPI: Mississippi Dept. of Wildlife Conservation, P.O. Box 451, Jackson, MS 39205

MISSOURI: Missouri Dept. of Conservation, P.O. Box 180, Jefferson City, MO 65101

MONTANA: Dept. of Fish, Wildlife and Parks, 1420 E. Sixth, Helena, MT 59620

NEBRASKA: Game and Parks Commission, 2200 N. 33d St., Box 30370, Lincoln, NB 68503

NEVADA: Dept. of Wildlife, Box 10678, Reno, NV 89520

NEW HAMPSHIRE: Fish and Game Dept., 35 Bridge St., Concord, NH 03301

NEW JERSEY: Division of Fish, Game and Wildlife, CN 400, Trenton, NJ 08625

NEW MEXICO: New Mexico Dept. of Game and Fish, Villagara Bldg., Santa Fe, NM 87503

NEW YORK: Wildlife Resources Center, Delmar, NY 12054

NORTH CAROLINA: North Carolina Resources Commission, Archdale Bldg., 512 N. Salisbury St., Raleigh, NC 27611

NORTH DAKOTA: Game and Fish Dept., 2121 Lovett Ave., Bismarck, ND 58505

OHIO: Dept. of Natural Resources, 1930 Belcher Dr., Fountain Square Bldg. C, Columbus, OH 43224

OKLAHOMA: Oklahoma Dept. of Wildlife Conservation, P.O. Box 53465, Oklahoma City, OK 73152

OREGON: Dept. of Fish and Wildlife, P.O. Box 3503, Portland, OR 97208

PENNSYLVANIA: Game Commission, P.O. Box 1567, Harrisburg, PA 17120

RHODE ISLAND: Division of Fish and Wildlife, Box 37, West Kingston, RI 02892

SOUTH CAROLINA: Wildlife and Marine Resources Dept., Rembert C. Dennis Bldg., P.O. Box 167, Columbia, SC 29202

SOUTH DAKOTA: Game, Fish and Parks Dept., Sigurd Anderson Bldg., Pierre, SD 57501

TENNESSEE: Tennessee Wildlife Resources Agency, Ellington Agriculture Center, P.O. Box 40747, Nashville, TN 37204

TEXAS: Texas Parks and Wildlife Dept., 4200 Smith School Rd., Austin, TX 78744

UTAH: Division of Wildlife Resources, 1596 W. North Temple, Salt Lake City, UT 84116

VERMONT: Fish and Game Dept., State Office Bldg., Montpelier, VT 05602

VIRGINIA: Commission of Game and Inland Fisheries, P.O. Box 11104, Richmond, VA 23230

WASHINGTON: Dept. of Game, 600 N. Capitol Way, Olympia, WA 98504

WEST VIRGINIA: Dept. of Natural Resources, 1800 E. Washington St., Charleston, WV 25305

WISCONSIN: Dept. of Wildlife, Box 7921, Madison, WI 53707

WYOMING: Game and Fish Dept., Cheyenne, WY 82002

Canada

ALBERTA: Alberta Fish and Wildlife Division, Natural Resources Bldg., 9833-109th St., Edmonton, Alberta T5K 2E1

BRITISH COLUMBIA: Environment and Land Use Commission, Parliament Bldg., Victoria, British Columbia V8V 1X4

Or: Dept. of Land, Forest and Water Resources, Parliament Bldg., Victoria, British Columbia V8V 1X4

MANITOBA: Dept. of Lands, Forests and Wildlife Resources, 9-989 Century St., Winnipeg, Manitoba R3H 0W4

NEWFOUNDLAND: Canadian Wildlife Service, Sir Humphrey Gilbert Bldg., Duckworth St., St. John's, Newfoundland A1C 1G4
Or: Dept. of Tourism, Wildlife Division, Confederation Building, 5th Floor, St. John's, Newfoundland

NORTHWEST TERRITORIES: Game Management Branch, Government of the Northwest Territories, Yellowknife, Northwest Territories

NOVA SCOTIA: Dept. of Environment, Box 2107, Halifax, Nova Scotia
Or: Dept. of Land and Forests, Dennis Bldg., Granville St., Halifax, Nova Scotia

ONTARIO: Wildlife Branch, Ministry of Natural Resources, Whitney Block, Toronto, Ontario M7A 1W3

PRINCE EDWARD ISLAND: Dept. of Fish and Wildlife, Environmental Control Commission, Box 2000, Charlottetown, Prince Edward Island, C1A 7N8

QUEBEC: Dept. of Tourism, Fish and Game, 150 St. Cyrille East, 15th Floor, Quebec, Quebec G1R 4Y3

SASKATCHEWAN: Dept. of Natural Resources, Fisheries and Wildlife Branch, Administrative Building, Regina, Saskatchewan S4S 0B1

YUKON TERRITORY: Game Branch, Government of the Yukon Territory, Whitehorse, Yukon Territory

Government Map Sources

CANADA

Map Distribution Office, Dept. of Mines and Technical Surveys, Ottawa, Ontario, Canada.
Canadian Government Travel Bureau, Ottawa, Ontario, Canada.

UNITED STATES

Branch of Distribution, U.S. Geological Survey, 1200 S. Eads St., Arlington, VA 22202. (Topographical maps and state indexes of maps for the United States east of the Mississippi River.)
Branch of Distribution, U.S. Geological Survey, Box 25286, Federal Center, Denver, CO 80255. (Topographical maps and state indexes of maps for the United States west of the Mississippi River.)
Bureau of Land Management, Dept. of the Interior, Washington, DC 20240.
U.S. Forest Service, Dept. of Agriculture, Washington, DC 20250
Bureau of Sport Fisheries and Wildlife, Washington, DC 20240. (For wilderness lands within National Wildlife Refuges and Ranges.)

Appendix 2

BALLISTICS TABLE
(Courtesy Remington Arms Co., Inc., Federal Cartridge Corp., and Winchester-Western)

CALIBERS	BULLET Wt.-Grs.	BULLET Style	VELOCITY FEET PER SECOND Muzzle	100 Yds.	200 Yds.	300 Yds.	400 Yds.	500 Yds.	ENERGY FOOT-POUNDS Muzzle	100 Yds.	200 Yds.	300 Yds.
17 Rem.	25	Hollow Point	4040	3284	2644	2086	1606	1235	906	599	388	242
22 Hornet	45	Pointed Soft Point	2690	2042	1502	1128	948	840	723	417	225	127
	45	Hollow Point	2690	2042	1502	1128	948	840	723	417	225	127
222 Rem.	50	Pointed Soft Point	3140	2602	2123	1700	1350	1107	1094	752	500	321
	50	Hollow Point	3140	2635	2182	1777	1432	1172	1094	771	529	351
	55	Metal Case	3020	2562	2147	1773	1451	1201	1114	801	563	384
222 Rem. Mag.	55	Pointed Soft Point	3240	2748	2305	1906	1556	1272	1282	922	649	444
	55	Hollow Point	3240	2773	2352	1969	1627	1341	1282	939	675	473
223 Rem.	55	Pointed Soft Point	3240	2747	2304	1905	1554	1270	1282	921	648	443
	55	Hollow Point	3240	2773	2352	1969	1627	1341	1282	939	675	473
	55	Metal Case	3240	2759	2326	1933	1587	1301	1282	929	660	456
22-250 Rem.	55	Pointed Soft Point	3730	3180	2695	2257	1863	1519	1699	1235	887	622
	55	Hollow Point	3730	3253	2826	2436	2079	1755	1699	1292	975	725
243 Win.	80	Pointed Soft Point	3350	2955	2593	2259	1951	1670	1993	1551	1194	906
	80	Hollow Point	3350	2955	2593	2259	1951	1670	1993	1551	1194	906
	100	Pointed Soft Point	2960	2697	2449	2215	1993	1786	1945	1615	1332	1089
6mm Rem.	80	Pointed Soft Point	3470	3064	2694	2352	2036	1747	2139	1667	1289	982
	80	Hollow Point	3470	3064	2694	2352	2036	1747	2139	1667	1289	982
	100	Pointed Soft Point	3130	2857	2600	2357	2127	1911	2175	1812	1501	1233
250 Savage	87	Pointed Soft Point	3030	2673	2342	2036	1755	1504	1773	1380	1059	801
	100	Pointed	2820	2467	2140	1839	1569	1339	1765	1351	1017	751
	60	Hollow Point	2760	2097	1542	1149	957	846	1015	586	317	176
256 Win. Mag.	87	Pointed Soft Point	3170	2802	2462	2147	1857	1594	1941	1516	1171	890
257 Roberts	100	Pointed	2900	2541	2210	1904	1627	1387	1867	1433	1084	805
	117	Pointed Soft Point	2650	2291	1961	1663	1404	1199	1824	1363	999	718
25-06 Rem.	87	Hollow Point	3440	2995	2591	2222	1884	1583	2286	1733	1297	954
	100	Pointed Soft Point	3230	2893	2580	2287	2014	1762	2316	1858	1478	1161
	120	Pointed Soft Point	3010	2749	2502	2269	2048	1840	2414	2013	1668	1372
6.5mm. Rem. Mag.	120	Pointed Soft Point	3210	2905	2621	2353	2102	1867	2745	2248	1830	1475
264 Win. Mag.	140	Pointed Soft Point	3030	2782	2548	2326	2114	1914	2854	2406	2018	1682
270 Win.	100	Pointed Soft Point	3480	3067	2690	2343	2023	1730	2689	2088	1606	1219
	130	Pointed Soft Point	3110	2823	2554	2300	2061	1837	2791	2300	1883	1527
	130	Pointed	3110	2849	2604	2371	2150	1941	2791	2343	1957	1622
	150	Soft Point	2900	2550	2225	1926	1653	1415	2801	2165	1649	1235
7mm Mauser	140	Pointed Soft Point	2660	2435	2221	2018	1827	1648	2199	1843	1533	1266
7mm-08 Rem.	140	Pointed Soft Point	2860	2625	2402	2189	1988	1798	2542	2142	1793	1490
280 Rem.	165	Soft Point	2820	2510	2220	1950	1701	1479	2913	2308	1805	1393
	150	Pointed Soft Point	2970	2699	2444	2203	1975	1763	2937	2426	1989	1616
284 Win.	125	Pointed Soft Point	3140	2829	2538	2265	2010	1772	2736	2221	1788	1424
	150	Pointed Soft Point	2860	2595	2344	2108	1886	1680	2724	2243	1830	1480

TRAJECTORY† 0.0 Indicates yardage at which rifle was sighted in.

ENERGY FOOT-POUNDS		SHORT RANGE Bullet does not rise more than one inch above line of sight from muzzle to sighting in range.						LONG RANGE Bullet does not rise more than three inches above line of sight from muzzle to sighting in range.							BARREL LENGTH
400 Yds.	500 Yds.	50 Yds.	100 Yds.	150 Yds.	200 Yds.	250 Yds.	300 Yds.	100 Yds.	150 Yds.	200 Yds.	250 Yds.	300 Yds.	400 Yds.	500 Yds.	
143	85	0.1	0.5	0.0	-1.5	-4.2	-8.5	2.1	2.5	1.9	-0.0	-3.4	-17.0	-44.3	24"
90	70	0.3	0.0	-2.4	-7.7	-16.9	-31.3	1.6	0.0	-4.5	-12.8	-26.4	-75.6	-163.4	24"
90	70	0.3	0.0	-2.4	-7.7	-16.9	-31.3	1.6	0.0	-4.5	-12.8	-26.4	-75.6	-161.4	
202	136	0.5	0.9	0.0	-2.5	-6.9	-13.7	2.2	1.9	0.0	-3.8	-10.0	-32.3	-73.8	
228	152	0.5	0.9	0.0	-2.4	-6.6	-13.1	2.1	1.8	0.0	-3.6	-9.5	-30.2	-68.1	24"
257	176	0.6	1.0	0.0	-2.5	-7.0	-13.7	2.2	1.9	0.0	-3.8	-9.9	-31.0	-68.7	
296	198	0.4	0.8	0.0	-2.2	-6.0	-11.8	1.9	1.6	0.0	-3.3	-8.5	-26.7	-59.5	24"
323	220	0.4	0.8	0.0	-2.1	-5.8	-11.4	1.8	1.6	0.0	-3.2	-8.2	-25.5	-56.0	
295	197	0.4	0.8	0.0	-2.2	-6.0	-11.8	1.9	1.6	0.0	-3.3	-8.5	-26.7	-59.6	
323	220	0.4	0.8	0.0	-2.1	-5.8	-11.4	1.8	1.6	0.0	-3.2	-8.2	-25.5	-56.0	24"
307	207	0.4	0.8	0.0	-2.1	-5.9	-11.6	1.9	1.6	0.0	-3.2	-8.4	-26.2	-57.9	
424	282	0.2	0.5	0.0	-1.5	-4.3	-8.4	2.2	2.6	1.9	0.0	-3.3	-15.4	-37.7	24"
528	376	0.2	0.5	0.0	-1.4	-4.0	-7.7	2.1	2.4	1.7	0.0·	-3.0	-13.6	-32.4	
676	495	0.3	0.7	0.0	-1.8	-4.9	-9.4	2.6	2.9	2.1	0.0	-3.6	-16.2	-37.9	
676	495	0.3	0.7	0.0	-1.8	-4.9	-9.4	2.6	2.9	2.1	0.0	-3.6	-16.2	-37.9	24"
882	708	0.5	0.9	0.0	-2.2	-5.8	-11.0	1.9	1.6	0.0	-3.1	-7.8	-22.6	-46.3	
736	542	0.3	0.6	0.0	-1.6	-4.5	-8.7	2.4	2.7	1.9	0.0	-3.3	-14.9	-35.0	
736	542	0.3	0.6	0.0	-1.6	-4.5	-8.7	2.4	2.7	1.9	0.0	-3.3	-14.9	-35.0	24"
1004	811	0.4	0.7	0.0	-1.9	-5.1	-9.7	1.7	1.4	0.0	-2.7	-6.8	-20.0	-40.8	
595	437	0.5	0.9	0.0	-2.3	-6.1	-11.8	2.0	1.7	0.0	-3.3	-8.4	-25.2	-53.4	24"
547	398	0.2	0.0	-1.6	-4.9	-10.0	-17.4	2.4	2.0	0.0	-3.9	-10.1	-30.5	-65.2	24"
122	95	0.3	0.0	-2.3	-7.3	-15.9	-29.6	1.5	0.0	-4.2	-12.1	-25.0	-72.1	-157.2	24"
666	491	0.4	0.8	0.0	-2.0	-5.5	-10.6	1.8	1.5	0.0	-3.0	-7.5	-22.7	-48.0	24"
588	427	0.6	1.0	0.0	-2.5	-6.9	-13.2	2.3	1.9	0.0	-3.7	-9.4	-28.6	-60.9	24"
512	373	0.3	0.0	-1.9	-5.8	-11.9	-20.7	2.9	2.4	0.0	-4.7	-12.0	-36.7	-79.2	24"
686	484	0.3	0.6	0.0	-1.7	-4.8	-9.3	2.5	2.9	2.1	0.0	-3.6	-16.4	-39.1	
901	689	0.4	0.7	0.0	-1.9	-5.0	-9.7	1.6	1.4	0.0	-2.7	-6.9	-20.5	-42.7	24"
1117	902	0.5	0.8	0.0	-2.1	-5.5	-10.5	1.9	1.6	0.0	-2.9	-7.4	-21.6	-44.2	
1177	929	0.4	0.7	0.0	-1.8	-4.9	-9.5	2.7	3.0	2.1	0.0	-3.5	-15.5	-35.3	24"
1389	1139	0.5	0.8	0.0	-2.0	-5.4	-10.2	1.8	1.5	0.0	-2.9	-7.2	-20.8	-42.2	24"
909	664	0.3	0.6	0.0	-1.6	-4.5	-8.7	2.4	2.7	1.9	0.0	-3.3	-15.0	-35.2	
1226	974	0.4	0.8	0.0	-2.0	-5.3	-10.0	1.7	1.5	0.0	-2.8	-7.1	-20.8	-42.7	24"
1334	1087	0.4	0.7	0.0	-1.9	-5.1	-9.7	1.7	1.4	0.0	-2.7	-6.8	-19.9	-40.5	
910	667	0.6	1.0	0.0	-2.5	-6.8	-13.1	2.2	1.9	0.0	-3.6	-9.3	-28.1	-59.7	
1037	844	0.2	0.0	-1.7	-5.0	-10.0	-17.0	2.5	2.0	0.0	-3.8	-9.6	-27.7	-56.3	24"
1228	1005	0.6	0.9	0.0	-2.3	-6.11	-11.6	2.1	1.7	0.0	-3.2	-8.1	-23.5	-47.7	24"
1060	801	0.2	0.0	-1.5	-4.6	-9.5	-16.4	2.3	1.9	0.0	-3.7	-9.4	-28.1	-58.8	24"
1299	1035	0.5	0.9	0.0	-2.2	-5.8	-11.0	1.9	1.6	0.0	-3.1	-7.8	-22.8	-46.7	24"
1121	871	0.4	0.8	0.0	-2.0	-6.3	-10.1	1.7	1.5	0.0	-2.8	-7.2	-21.1	-43.7	24"
1185	940	0.6	1.0	0.0	-2.4	-6.3	-12.1	2.1	1.8	0.0	-3.4	-8.5	-24.8	-51.0	24"

BALLISTICS TABLE

(Courtesy Remington Arms Co., Inc., Federal Cartridge Corp., and Winchester-Western)

CALIBERS	BULLET Wt.-Grs.	BULLET Style	VELOCITY FEET PER SECOND Muzzle	100 Yds.	200 Yds.	300 Yds.	400 Yds.	500 Yds.	ENERGY FOOT-POUNDS Muzzle	100 Yds.	200 Yds.	300 Yds.
7mm Rem. Mag.	125	Pointed Soft Point	3310	2976	2666	2376	2105	1852	3040	2458	1972	1567
	150	Pointed Soft Point	3110	2830	2568	2320	2085	1866	3221	2667	2196	1792
	175	Pointed Soft Point	2860	2645	2440	2244	2057	1879	3178	2718	2313	1956
30 Carbine	110	Soft Point	1990	1567	1236	1035	923	842	967	600	373	262
30 Rem.	170	Soft Point	2120	1822	1555	1328	1153	1036	1696	1253	913	666
30-30 Win. Accelerator	55	Soft Point	3400	2693	2085	1570	1187	986	1412	886	521	301
30-30 Win.	150	Soft Point	2390	1973	1605	1303	1095	974	1902	1296	858	565
	170	Soft Point	2200	1895	1619	1381	1191	1061	1827	1355	989	720
	170	Hollow Point	2200	1895	1619	1381	1191	1061	1827	1355	989	720
30-06 Springfield Accelerator	55	Pointed Soft Point	4080	3485	2965	2502	2083	1709	2033	1483	1074	754
30-06 Springfield	110	Pointed Soft Point	3380	2843	2365	1936	1561	1261	2790	1974	1366	915
	125	Pointed Soft Point	3140	2780	2447	2138	1853	1595	2736	2145	1662	1269
	150	Pointed Soft Point	2910	2617	2342	2083	1843	1622	2820	2281	1827	1445
	150	Pointed	2910	2656	2416	2189	1974	1773	2820	2349	1944	1596
	165	Pointed Soft Point	2800	2534	2283	2047	1825	1621	2872	2352	1909	1534
	180	Soft Point	2700	2348	2023	1727	1466	1251	2913	2203	1635	1192
	180	Pointed Soft Point	2700	2469	2250	2042	1846	1663	2913	2436	2023	1666
	180	Bronze Point	2700	2485	2280	2084	1899	1725	2913	2468	2077	1736
	200	Boat-tail Soft Point	2550	2400	2260	2120	1990	1860	2890	2560	2270	2000
	220	Soft Point	2410	2130	1870	1632	1422	1246	2837	2216	1708	1301
30-40 Krag	180	Pointed Soft Point	2430	2099	1795	1525	1298	1128	2360	1761	1288	929
	180	Pointed	2430	2213	2007	1813	1632	1468	2360	1957	1610	1314
	220	Pointed	2160	1956	1765	1587	1427	1287	2279	1869	1522	1230
300 Win. Mag.	150	Pointed Soft Point	3290	2951	2636	2342	2068	1813	3605	2900	2314	1827
	180	Pointed Soft Point	2960	2745	2540	2344	2157	1979	3501	3011	2578	2196
	220	Pointed	2680	2448	2228	2020	1823	1640	3508	2927	2424	1993
300 H.&H. Mag.	150	Pointed	3130	2822	2534	2264	2011	1776	3262	2652	2138	1707
	180	Pointed	2880	2640	2412	2196	1991	1798	3315	2785	2325	1927
	220	Pointed	2580	2341	2114	1901	1702	1520	3251	2677	2183	1765
300 Savage	150	Pointed Soft Point	2630	2311	2015	1743	1500	1295	2303	1779	1352	1012
	150	Pointed	2630	2354	2095	1853	1631	1484	2303	1845	1462	1143
	180	Pointed Soft Point	2350	2025	1728	1467	1252	1098	2207	1639	1193	860
	180	Pointed	2350	2137	1935	1745	1570	1413	2207	1825	1496	1217
303 Savage	190	Pointed	1940	1657	1410	1211	1073	982	1588	1158	839	619
303 British	180	Pointed Soft Point	2460	2233	2018	1816	1629	1459	2418	1993	1627	1318
307 Win.	150	Soft Point	2760	2321	1924	1575	1289	1091	2538	1795	1233	826
	180	Soft Point	2510	2179	1874	1599	1362	1177	2519	1898	1404	1022
308 Win Accelerator	55	Pointed Soft Point	3770	3215	2726	2286	1888	1541	1735	1262	907	638

TRAJECTORY† 0.0 Indicates yardage at which rifle was sighted in.

ENERGY FOOT-POUNDS		SHORT RANGE — Bullet does not rise more than one inch above line of sight from muzzle to sighting in range.						LONG RANGE — Bullet does not rise more than three inches above line of sight from muzzle to sighting in range.							BARREL LENGTH
400 Yds.	500 Yds.	50 Yds.	100 Yds.	150 Yds.	200 Yds.	250 Yds.	300 Yds.	100 Yds.	150 Yds.	200 Yds.	250 Yds.	300 Yds.	400 Yds.	500 Yds.	
1230	952	0.3	0.6	0.0	−1.7	−4.7	−9.1	2.5	2.8	2.0	0.0	−3.4	−15.0	−34.5	24″
1448	1160	0.4	0.8	0.0	−1.9	−5.2	−9.9	1.7	1.5	0.0	−2.8	−7.0	−20.5	−42.1	24″
1644	1372	0.6	0.9	0.0	−2.3	−6.0	−11.3	2.0	1.7	0.0	−3.2	−7.9	−22.7	−45.8	24″
208	173	0.9	0.0	−4.5	−13.5	−28.3	−49.9	0.0	−4.5	−13.5	−28.3	−49.9	−118.6	−228.2	20″
502	405	0.7	0.0	−3.3	−9.7	−19.6	−33.8	2.2	0.0	−5.3	−14.1	−27.2	−69.0	−136.9	24″
172	119	0.4	0.8	0.0	−2.4	−6.7	−13.8	2.0	1.8	0.0	−3.8	−10.2	−35.0	−84.4	24″
399	316	0.5	0.0	−2.7	−8.2	−17.0	−30.0	1.8	0.0	−4.6	−12.5	−24.6	−65.3	−134.9	
535	425	0.6	0.0	−3.0	−8.9	−18.0	−31.1	2.0	0.0	−4.8	−13.0	−25.1	−63.6	−126.7	24″
535	425	0.6	0.0	−3.0	−8.9	−18.0	−31.1	2.0	0.0	−4.8	−13.0	−25.1	−63.6	−126.7	
550	356	0.4	1.0	0.9	0.0	−1.9	−5.0	1.8	2.1	1.5	−0.0	−2.7	−12.5	−30.5	24″
595	388	0.4	0.7	0.0	−2.0	−5.6	−11.1	1.7	1.5	0.0	−3.1	−8.0	−25.5	−57.4	24″
953	706	0.4	0.8	0.0	−2.1	−5.6	−10.7	1.8	1.5	0.0	−3.0	−7.7	−23.0	−48.5	
1131	876	0.6	0.9	0.0	−2.3	−6.3	−12.0	2.1	1.8	0.0	−3.3	−8.5	−25.0	−51.8	
1298	1047	0.6	0.9	0.0	−2.2	−6.0	−11.4	2.0	1.7	0.0	−3.2	−8.0	−23.3	−47.5	
1220	963	0.7	1.0	0.0	−2.5	−6.7	−12.7	2.3	1.9	0.0	−3.6	−9.0	−26.3	−54.1	24″
859	625	0.2	0.0	−1.8	−5.5	−11.2	−19.5	2.7	2.3	0.0	−4.4	−11.3	−34.4	−73.7	
1362	1105	0.2	0.0	−1.6	−4.8	−9.7	−16.5	2.4	2.0	0.0	−3.7	−9.3	−27.0	−54.9	
1441	1189	0.2	0.0	−1.6	−4.7	−9.6	−16.2	2.4	2.0	0.0	−3.6	−9.1	−26.2	−53.0	
1760	1540	0.6	0.0	−2.7	−6.0	−12.4	−18.8	2.3	1.8	0.0	−4.1	−9.0	−25.8	−51.3	
988	758	0.4	0.0	−2.3	−6.8	−13.8	−23.6	1.5	0.0	−3.7	−9.9	−19.0	−47.4	−93.1	
673	508	0.4	0.0	−2.4	−7.1	−14.5	−25.0	1.6	0.0	−3.9	−10.5	−20.3	−51.7	−103.9	
1064	861	0.4	0.0	−2.1	−6.2	−12.5	−21.1	1.4	0.0	−3.4	−8.9	−16.8	−40.9	−78.1	
995	809	0.6	0.0	−2.9	−8.2	−16.4	−27.6	1.9	0.0	−4.4	−11.6	−21.9	−53.3	−101.8	
1424	1095	0.3	0.7	0.0	−1.8	−4.8	−9.3	2.6	2.9	2.1	0.0	−3.5	−15.4	−35.5	
1859	1565	0.5	0.8	0.0	−2.2	−5.5	−10.4	1.9	1.6	0.0	−2.9	−7.3	−20.9	−41.9	
1623	1314	0.2	0.0	−1.7	−4.9	−9.9	−16.9	2.5	2.0	0.0	−3.8	−9.5	−27.5	−56.1	
1347	1050	0.4	0.8	0.0	−2.0	−5.3	−10.1	1.7	1.5	0.0	−2.8	−7.2	−21.2	−43.8	
1584	1292	0.6	0.9	0.0	−2.3	−6.0	−11.5	2.1	1.7	0.0	−3.2	−8.0	−23.3	−47.4	
1415	1128	0.3	0.0	−1.9	−5.5	−11.0	−18.7	2.7	2.2	0.0	−4.2	−10.5	−30.7	−63.0	
749	558	0.3	0.0	−1.9	−5.7	−11.6	−19.9	2.8	2.3	0.0	−4.5	−11.5	−34.4	−73.0	
886	685	0.3	0.0	−1.8	−5.4	−11.0	−18.8	2.7	2.2	0.0	−4.2	−10.7	−31.5	−65.5	
626	482	0.5	0.0	−2.6	−7.7	−15.6	−27.1	1.7	0.0	−4.2	−11.3	−21.9	−55.8	−112.0	
985	798	0.4	0.0	−2.3	−6.7	−13.5	−22.8	1.5	0.0	−3.6	−9.6	−18.2	−44.1	−84.2	
486	407	0.9	0.0	−4.1	−11.9	−24.1	−41.4	2.7	0.0	−6.4	−17.3	−33.2	−83.7	−164.4	
1060	851	0.3	0.0	−2.1	−6.1	−12.2	−20.8	1.4	0.0	−3.3	−8.8	−16.6	−40.4	−77.4	
554	397	0.2	0.0	−1.9	−5.6	−11.8	−20.8	1.2	0.0	−3.2	−8.7	−17.1	−44.9	−92.2	24″
742	554	0.3	0.0	−2.2	−6.5	−13.3	−22.9	1.5	0.0	−3.6	−9.6	−18.6	−47.1	−93.7	24″
435	290	0.2	0.5	0.0	−1.5	−4.2	−8.2	2.2	2.5	1.8	−0.0	−3.2	−15.0	−36.7	24″

BALLISTICS TABLE

(Courtesy Remington Arms Co., Inc., Federal Cartridge Corp., and Winchester-Western)

CALIBERS	BULLET		VELOCITY FEET PER SECOND						ENERGY FOOT-POUNDS			
	Wt.-Grs.	Style	Muzzle	100 Yds.	200 Yds.	300 Yds.	400 Yds.	500 Yds.	Muzzle	100 Yds.	200 Yds.	300 Yds.
308 Win.	110	Pointed Soft Point	3180	2666	2206	1795	1444	1178	2470	1736	1188	787
	125	Pointed Soft Point	3050	2697	2370	2067	1788	1537	2582	2019	1559	1186
	150	Pointed Soft Point	2820	2533	2263	2009	1774	1560	2648	2137	1705	1344
	180	Soft Point	2620	2274	1955	1666	1414	1212	2743	2066	1527	1109
	180	Pointed Soft Point	2620	2393	2178	1974	1782	1604	2743	2288	1896	1557
	165	Boat-tail Soft Point	2700	2520	2330	2160	1990	1830	2670	2310	1990	1700
32-20 Win.	100	Lead	1210	1021	913	834	769	712	325	231	185	154
	100	Soft Point	1210	1021	913	834	769	712	325	231	185	154
32 Win. Special	170	Soft Point	2250	1921	1626	1372	1175	1044	1911	1393	998	710
8mm Mauser	170	Soft Point	2360	1969	1622	1333	1123	997	2102	1463	993	671
8mm Rem. Mag.	185	Pointed Soft Point	3080	2761	2464	2186	1927	1688	3896	3131	2494	1963
	220	Pointed Soft Point	2830	2581	2346	2123	1913	1716	3912	3254	2688	2201
338 Win. Mag.	200	Pointed Soft Point	2960	2658	2375	2110	1862	1635	3890	3137	2505	1977
	225	Pointed Soft Point	2780	2572	2374	2184	2003	1832	3862	3306	2816	2384
	250	Pointed	2660	2395	2145	1910	1693	1497	3927	3184	2554	2025
348 Win.	200	Pointed	2520	2215	1931	1672	1443	1253	2820	2178	1656	1241
35 Rem.	150	Pointed Soft Point	2300	1874	1506	1218	1039	934	1762	1169	755	494
	200	Soft Point	2080	1698	1376	1140	1001	911	1921	1280	841	577
356 Win.	200	Soft Point	2460	2114	1797	1517	1284	1113	2688	1985	1434	1022
	250	Soft Point	2160	1911	1682	1476	1299	1158	2591	2028	1571	1210
350 Rem. Mag.	200	Pointed Soft Point	2710	2410	2130	1870	1631	1421	3261	2579	2014	1553
358 Win.	200	Pointed	2490	2171	1876	1610	1379	1194	2753	2093	1563	1151
	250	Pointed	2230	1988	1762	1577	1375	1224	2760	2194	1723	1346
375 Win.	200	Pointed Soft Point	2200	1841	1526	1268	1089	980	2150	1506	1034	714
	250	Pointed Soft Point	1900	1647	1424	1239	1103	1011	2005	1506	1126	852
375 H.&H. Mag.	270	Soft Point	2690	2420	2166	1928	1707	1507	4337	3510	2812	2228
	300	Metal Case	2530	2171	1843	1551	1307	1126	4263	3139	2262	1602
44-40 Win.	200	Soft Point	1190	1006	900	822	756	699	629	449	360	300
44 Rem. Mag.	240	Soft Point	1760	1380	1114	970	878	806	1650	1015	661	501
	240	Semi-Jacketed Hollow Point	1760	1380	1114	970	878	806	1650	1015	661	501
444 Mar.	240	Soft Point	2350	1815	1377	1087	941	846	2942	1755	1010	630
	265	Soft Point	2120	1733	1405	1160	1012	920	2644	1768	1162	791
45-70 Government	405	Soft Point	1330	1168	1055	977	918	869	1590	1227	1001	858
458 Win. Mag.	500	Metal Case	2040	1823	1623	1442	1237	1161	4628	3689	2924	2308
	510	Soft Point	2040	1770	1527	1319	1157	1046	4712	3547	2640	1970

TRAJECTORY† 0.0 Indicates yardage at which rifle was sighted in.

ENERGY FOOT-POUNDS		SHORT RANGE Bullet does not rise more than one inch above line of sight from muzzle to sighting in range.						LONG RANGE Bullet does not rise more than three inches above line of sight from muzzle to sighting in range.							BARREL LENGTH
400 Yds.	500 Yds.	50 Yds.	100 Yds.	150 Yds.	200 Yds.	250 Yds.	300 Yds.	100 Yds.	150 Yds.	200 Yds.	250 Yds.	300 Yds.	400 Yds.	500 Yds.	
509	339	0.5	0.9	0.0	−2.3	−6.5	−12.8	2.0	1.8	0.0	−3.5	−9.3	−29.5	−66.7	
887	656	0.5	0.8	0.0	−2.2	−6.0	−11.5	2.0	1.7	0.0	−3.2	−8.2	−24.6	−51.9	
1048	810	0.2	0.0	−1.5	−4.5	−9.3	−15.9	2.3	1.9	0.0	−3.6	−9.1	−26.9	−55.7	
799	587	0.3	0.0	−2.0	−5.9	−12.1	−20.9	2.9	2.4	0.0	−4.7	−12.1	−36.9	−79.1	24″
1269	1028	0.2	0.0	−1.8	−5.2	−10.4	−17.7	2.6	2.1	0.0	−4.0	−9.9	−28.9	−58.8	
1450	1230	1.3	0.0	−1.3	−4.0	−8.4	−14.4	2.0	1.7	0.0	−3.3	−8.4	−24.8	−48.9	
131	113	0.0	−6.3	−20.9	−44.9	−79.3	−125.1	0.0	−11.5	−32.3	−63.8	−106.3	−230.3	−413.3	24″
131	113	0.0	−6.3	−20.9	−44.9	−79.3	−125.1	0.0	−11.5	−32.3	−63.6	−106.3	−230.3	−413.3	
521	411	0.6	0.0	−2.9	−8.6	−17.6	−30.5	1.9	0.0	−4.7	−12.7	−24.7	−63.2	−126.9	24″
476	375	0.5	0.0	−2.7	−8.2	−17.0	−29.8	1.8	0.0	−4.5	−12.4	−24.3	−63.8	−130.7	24″
1525	1170	0.5	0.8	0.0	−2.1	−5.6	−10.7	1.8	1.6	0.0	−3.0	−7.6	−22.5	−46.8	24″
1787	1438	0.6	1.0	0.0	−2.4	−6.4	−12.1	2.2	1.8	0.0	−3.4	−8.5	−24.7	−50.5	
1539	1187	0.5	0.9	0.0	−2.3	−6.1	−11.6	2.0	1.7	0.0	−3.2	−8.2	−24.3	−50.4	
2005	1677	1.2	1.3	0.0	−2.7	−7.1	−12.9	2.7	2.1	0.0	−3.6	−9.4	−25.0	−49.9	
1591	1244	0.2	0.0	−1.7	−5.2	−10.5	−18.0	2.6	2.1	0.0	−4.0	−10.2	−30.0	−61.9	
925	697	0.3	0.0	−2.1	−6.2	−12.7	−21.9	1.4	0.0	−3.4	−9.2	−17.7	−44.4	−87.9	
359	291	0.6	0.0	−3.0	−9.2	−19.1	−33.9	2.0	0.0	−5.1	−14.1	−27.8	−74.0	−152.3	24″
445	369	0.8	0.0	−3.8	−11.3	−23.5	−41.2	2.5	0.0	−6.3	−17.1	−33.6	−87.7	−176.4	
732	550	0.4	0.0	−2.3	−7.0	−14.3	−24.7	1.6	0.0	−3.8	−10.4	−20.1	−51.2	−102.3	24″
937	745	0.6	0.0	−3.0	−8.7	−17.4	−30.0	2.0	0.0	−4.7	−12.4	−23.7	−58.4	−112.9	24″
1181	897	0.2	0.0	−1.7	−5.1	−10.4	−17.9	2.6	2.1	0.0	−4.0	−10.3	−30.5	−64.0	20″
844	633	0.4	0.0	−2.2	−6.5	−13.3	−23.0	1.5	0.0	−3.6	−9.7	−18.6	−47.2	−94.1	24″
1049	832	0.5	0.0	−2.7	−7.9	−16.0	−27.1	1.8	0.0	−4.3	−11.4	−21.7	−53.5	−103.7	24″
527	427	0.6	0.0	−3.2	−9.5	−19.5	−33.8	2.1	0.0	−5.2	−14.1	−27.4	−70.1	−138.1	24″
676	568	0.9	0.0	−4.1	−12.0	−24.0	−40.9	2.7	0.0	−6.5	−17.2	−32.7	−80.6	−154.1	24″
1747	1361	0.2	0.0	−1.7	−5.1	−10.3	−17.6	2.5	2.1	0.0	−3.9	−10.0	−29.4	−60.7	24″
1138	844	0.3	0.0	−2.2	−6.5	−13.5	−23.4	1.5	0.0	−3.6	−9.8	−19.1	−49.1	−99.5	
254	217	0.0	−6.5	−21.6	−46.3	−81.8	−129.1	0.0	−11.8	−33.3	−65.5	−109.5	−237.4	−426.2	24″
411	346	0.0	−2.7	−10.0	−23.0	−43.0	−71.2	0.0	−5.9	−17.6	−36.3	−63.1	−145.5	−273.0	20″
411	346	0.0	−2.7	−10.0	−23.0	−43.0	−71.2	0.0	−5.9	−17.6	−36.3	−63.1	−145.5	−273.0	
472	381	0.6	0.0	−3.2	−9.9	−21.3	−38.5	2.1	0.0	−5.6	−15.9	−32.1	−87.8	−182.7	24″
603	498	0.7	0.0	−3.6	−10.8	−22.5	−39.5	2.4	0.0	−6.0	−16.4	−32.2	−84.3	−170.2	
758	679	0.0	−4.7	−15.8	−34.0	−60.0	−94.5	0.0	−8.7	24.6	−48.2	−80.3	−172.4	−305.9	24″
1839	1469	0.7	0.0	−3.3	−9.6	−19.2	−32.5	2.2	0.0	−5.2	−13.6	−25.8	−63.2	−121.7	24″
1516	1239	0.8	0.0	−3.5	−10.3	−20.8	−35.6	2.4	0.0	−5.6	−14.9	−28.5	−71.5	−140.4	